THE IMPACT OF
AMERICAN CONSTITUTIONALISM
ABROAD

*The Gaspar G. Bacon Lecture
on the Constitution
of the United States*

1966

THE IMPACT
OF AMERICAN
CONSTITUTIONALISM
ABROAD

Carl J. Friedrich

BOSTON UNIVERSITY PRESS

BOSTON, MASSACHUSETTS

1967

To
Roger Nash Baldwin
Champion of Universal
Human Rights

"We need not hope in order to act,
    nor to succeed in order to persevere."

WILLIAM OF ORANGE

The Bacon Lectureship

The Gaspar G. Bacon Lectureship on the Constitution of the United States was established in 1927 by Mrs. Robert Bacon of New York in honor of her son, at that time Secretary of the Board of Trustees of Boston University. After several terms in the Massachusetts General Court (legislature) and two years as Lieutenant Governor, Gaspar G. Bacon retired from active politics and joined the Department of Government, College of Liberal Arts at Boston University in 1938. His teaching career was interrupted by four years of service in World War II. September 1947 found Professor Bacon back at Boston University, but only for a short period which ended suddenly with his death on Christmas Day.

Since 1927 the Bacon Lectures have been given annually by an eminent scholar or jurist in fulfillment of the terms of the deed of gift which reads, "The purpose of the Lectureship is to stimulate a study of the Constitution of the United States, its antecedents, history and doctrine, together with the results and implications thereof."

CONTENTS

CHAPTER I

REFLECTIONS ON THE
INFLUENCE OF
AMERICAN IDEAS

That American constitutionalism has had a powerful impact upon political institutions elsewhere is beyond the peradventure of a doubt. But what this influence has been is very difficult to determine.[1] The channels through which ideas flow are very numerous. Through books and articles, through personal contact and observation, true knowledge as well as quite erroneous impressions and outright prejudices, are transmitted from one country to another. Since the days of the founders, Americans have been protesting against what they believed to be highly misleading notions about their country and its institutions. John Adams, when asked by two leading French intellectuals for help in writing a history of the American Revolution, after giving them a long list of documents, warned them against existing writings: "All these histories [on the American War and the American Revolution] both in French and English, are only monuments of the complete ignorance of the writers of their subject." While typically Adamsian in its acidity, this comment shows how twisted was the image and hence the impact of American ideas.[2]

It would seem that the impact of American constitutionalism can be roughly divided into three periods: the early period of general enthusiasm after the adoption of the Constitution, a middle period highlighted by the constitution-making of 1848, and a late period following the two world wars and their extensive constitutionalizing of previously autocratic regimes. In each of these periods, one book seems to have played a primary role as *the* interpreter of the American political order: *The Federalist* in the first, Tocqueville's *Democracy in America* in the second, and James Bryce's *American Commonwealth* in the third, although after World War II, due to the participation of numerous American political scientists in the discussions about the new constitutions the impact becomes at once diffuse and ubiquitous.

Generally speaking, these three periods are quite distinct, as far as the positive impact is concerned. During the first, the widely felt enthusiasm for the American republic among all those with republican and democratic sentiments in Europe—for the impact at that time is strictly limited to Europe—was coupled with a sense of distance. Goethe's celebrated exclamation: "Amerika, Du hast es besser" poetically expressed a widespread feeling that America was too different to serve as a model, that its lack of monarchy, of feudal classes, its wide open frontier (really the absence of a boundary in the European political sense), that all these and the variegated population from many lands made the American experiment both exciting and unique, but inimitable. After a half century of stabilization, during which the United States had become a well-functioning political order, its institutional framework, and more especially its federalism, seemed on the contrary to offer wide opportunities for providing an example worthy of emulation, if not in its entirety, then at any rate in some of its institutions.

Curiously, but quite understandably, its key institution, namely the presidency, was generally rejected, the reason being that it seemed too close to the monarchy which most of the constitutionalists were seeking to eliminate. The only exception was Latin America. Here, too, the British parliamentary system had a stronger appeal in a number of countries, such as Argentina. But there were others which adopted the presidential system; and even those which at first had rejected it, gradually either drifted into it, like Argentina, or explicitly adopted it, like Brazil. But Latin America apart, there can be little question that the presidential system, while always having advocates, did not win out until very recently. Federalism and basic rights on the other hand seemed worthy of close attention, and their implementing guardian, judicial review, subjects of keen concern and lively debate.

The American Civil War, rightly considered the most formidable military confrontation of the century, put an end to the largely uncritical admiration of American constitutionalism. By the turn of the century, a new sense of distance spread abroad. By now America had become so powerful, its industrial might loomed as so extraordinary, and its continental reach seemed so formidable that once again the feeling spread that America could not serve as a model for a limited national state. Thus in the third period, although discussions of American institutions filled the records of constitutional debates and conventions after both world wars, the general feeling was that America was different. Such an attitude was reinforced by the fact that many of the constitution-makers were socialists and as such were repelled by the rampant capitalism of the United States and its corrupting influence in politics.

American politics after 1900 becomes linked with Tammany Hall, and hence acquires a jaded aspect. Not only Bryce's candid descriptions, but also the writings of the muckrakers deeply influenced foreign opinion.[3] This gen-

5

eral trend was, of course, very much intensified after 1917. Since the Bolshevik revolution in Russia, European thought has been increasingly shaped by the hostile view of the United States prevalent among intellectuals who, if not necessarily Communists, inclined to sympathize with the Soviet Union. A perhaps grotesque instance of this attitude was the book by Sidney and Beatrice Webb, *The Truth about Soviet Russia,* published in the midst of World War II, and culminating in the proposition that the Soviet Union is the true democracy, "the most inclusive and equalized democracy, in the world," and that Stalin is not only not a dictator, but that "the presiding member of the Sovnarkom has not anything like the autocratic power of the president of the United States." [4] Views of this sort were then, and have been since, frequently voiced in those circles which are the protagonists of radical democracy in Europe and throughout Asia, Africa, and Latin America. Roosevelt "the virtual dictator of the United States" could not but frighten constitution-makers who wished to escape the autocracy of a Mussolini, a Hitler, and the rest.

This is indeed a different setting from that of the eighteenth and early nineteenth centuries when a Dr. Priestley could write to Burke: "The Americans . . . set a glorious example to France, and to the world. They formed a completely new government on the principles of equal liberty and the rights of men." [5] There was almost universal enthusiasm for the American enterprise among forward looking people. It was part of the revolutionary spirit which was sweeping intellectual circles as a culmination of the age of reason and enlightenment.[6] But while the French revolutionaries readily assumed that their plans were valid for all peoples and their constitutions a model of a political order for any free nation, the Americans were more sober and inclined to take the view that what was possible in America need not be possible elsewhere. This sentiment was widely shared among visitors to the United States. The same Dr. Priestley who had so unqualifiedly welcomed the "glorious example" which America was giving, later after a visit, reported, in his *Lectures on History and General Policy,* that the revolution in America had been easy, because "there never had been any nobility in the country, no hereditary power of any kind, nor any general establishment of religion," and hence very few things had to be changed.[7] It was only a short step from this notion of an easy revolution in which little change occurred to Tocqueville's more famous assertion that there had been no revolution at all.[8]

Such a view is far removed from how leading Americans understood and interpreted their own enterprise. The institutions which were finally adopted were by their framers considered distinct innovations. In the fourteenth chapter of *The Federalist,* James Madison stated this sense of novelty very emphatically. After speaking of the "numerous innovations" which the convention had worked out, he exclaimed: "They [the drafters of the constitution] accomplished a revolution which has no parallel in the annals of human society. They reared the fabrics of governments which have no model on the face of the globe." He was right, and in the political perspective the revolution was real, indeed. Our time more readily understands this fact than did Tocqueville. Within the context of Western society, the Americans established the framework for an ongoing revolution, a "permanent revolution," as it were.[9] Revolutionizing impulses which have been generated by the American "experiment" have served to transform Western, and indeed world, civilization. Nor are the revolutionary potentialities of American constitutionalism by any means exhausted. They are still at work both in the United States and abroad.

7

Among these impulses the strictly constitutional ones, while important, are by no means the only ones. In this brief study we nonetheless propose to concentrate upon them. It is not an easy task. We must choose some key aspects of American constitutionalism and deal with them selectively. We have chosen presidentialism, federalism and "judicialism," that is the particular form of judicial guardianship of the Constitution and more especially of the human rights guaranteed by it. Each of these constitutes a key feature of American constitutionalism; that is to say they are such vital parts of the American political system that without any one of them, the system could not survive. There might still be a mighty American nation calling itself the United States, but it would not be the system organized in 1787.[10]

These three vital features of American constitutionalism have had a divergent impact. As we hope to show, the story for each of them is quite distinct. Rarely has an attempt been made to adopt the American system in its entirety, save for minor adaptations. The closest case is perhaps that of the Brazilian constitution of 1891. The fact that the impact is thus segmented and fragmented is responsible for its inconclusiveness. Torn from context, particular American institutions may function very differently and fail to give the results which they produced in their native habitat. It is an arguable position that once the systemic links have been disrupted, the institution is no longer the same, and can therefore not fairly be cited as a case of genuine impact. It is arguable; but we are planning to work here with the opposite hypothesis.

Broadly sketched, the contrast between the impact of the three principles is this. Presidentialism, while often discussed and sometimes advocated, was adopted only in some states of Latin America. In Europe, there was always the fear that presidentialism would turn into dictatorship, and the events in France under the two Napoleons served to reinforce this fear. It was also often argued, as we hope to show in greater detail in a later chapter, that the American presidency was fashioned in the image of the British monarchy, because at the time parliamentary cabinet government had not yet been recognized as the emergent form of English constitutionalism; the particular separation of powers, dividing the executive from the legislative function was believed by many to be an eighteenth-century notion, superseded by the new form of executive-legislative relation. It is only in recent years and in the light of increasing difficulties encountered especially by the French version of parliamentary government that the idea of presidentialism has been gaining ground.

Federalism, by contrast, was readily recognized as a distinctive American solution to a problem confronting many countries. Not only in Switzerland and Germany, where ancient confederal orders were proving increasingly inadequate, but also in many other contexts the notion of an integrated federal order, of a "federal state," was welcomed, especially after it had proved its viability during a half century of steady growth of the United States. The set-back which this widespread acclaim suffered as a result of the American Civil War—manifestly a breakdown of the American federal order—soon was overcome as the United States proved not only to have weathered this dangerous crisis, but also to have emerged stronger and more dynamic than when she entered it. America's industrial progress after the Civil War was the first *Wirtschaftswunder,* comparable in many ways to the German one after 1945. Therefore the paradigmatic impact of American federalism continued, eventually even helping to shape international orders.

On human rights and their judicial protection, the story

is again a different one. The French Declaration has such a wide influence and is so intimately intertwined with the American ones—a number of state constitutions developing, of course, elaborate bills quite a few years before both the French Declaration and the American amendments—that it is impossible to disentangle the story. But when we turn to judicialism, we find that the reluctance to adopt it was very great. Only in very recent years, essentially since the end of World War II, has the general idea been spreading. Yet again, the American model has been so widely deviated from and thus so greatly altered, that the candid observer is obliged to wonder what the impact eventually will be.

The entire story is, of course, basically affected by one's views as to the possibility of transmitting political institutions. The deep-seated romantic view, superbly stated by Burke and the historical school, is that no such transfer is possible at all. "Si duo faciunt idem, non est idem"—and it is of course true that in one very real sense nothing is ever the same. Not only when two do the same thing is it not the same, but when the same person does the same thing it is not the same. Political institutions are continually undergoing transformation, and the transmission of a political institution will necessarily occur in the light of the understanding which men have of that institution at an earlier period than the one when the transmission occurs. The American presidency, American federalism, and the Supreme Court have undergone very significant alterations in the course of history, many of them not fully appreciated in their portent at the time the discussion occurred. And yet, it is also a fact that in the field of political institutions, as in other fields of culture, transmission does occur. With all due allowance for the inadequacy of abstractions from the concrete reality, these abstractions have a definite meaning and significance. The diffusion of political institutions and processes will necessarily take this form. Indeed, the American Constitution itself is a striking instance of such adaptation. "It is common misunderstanding," we wrote some years ago in dealing with the roots of American constitutionalism, "to think that great historical events, such as the Declaration of Independence and the efforts at constitution-making which followed it, spring from social life and man's initiative like Athene from the forehead of Zeus. In point of fact, events of this type have a long seed time." [11] The American Constitution is a skillful weaving together of many strands of political thought and experience, stretching from the Old Testament and Greek philosophy down to the theories and practices of the immediate forebears of the men of the American Revolution. If political thought and institutions could not be transmitted, as an excessive scepticism would have us believe, no American Constitution would ever have seen the light of day.

At the same time, it seems that particular features of a system of institutions, torn from their context of living relations, rarely function in the same way within the new context to which they have been transplanted. Hence their impact is a curiously twisted and paradoxical one. The breadth of the Constitution's theoretical base, including its built-in contradictions, has facilitated the assimilation of particular features into radically different constitutional systems. Wherever men have gathered to draft a constitution, they have drawn upon American constitutional theory and practice. The attentive student of these constitutional debates is often forced to conclude that American constitutionalism's greatest impact occurred *not* by way of having American institutions taken over lock, stock, and barrel, but by stimulating men into thinking out the various alternatives confronting them.

Among these alternatives, the most important and to

many the more alluring has been the British constitutional order. American constitutionalism, though fundamentally derived from the British constitutional tradition, is in many ways its dialectical antithesis. Where the British constitution is a complex of laws, customs, and changing ways of behaving, the American Constitution is at the outset a formal document, carefully thought out in all its parts and seeking to construct a *rational* whole.[12] Its rationalism strongly contrasts with British traditionalism—a second antithesis. But the antitheses are much more numerous. Where the British constitution closely links executive and legislative authority, the American separates and balances them in its presidential system. Where the British constitution is strongly centralist, in spite of its tradition of local government, the American is distinguished by its federalism. Judicial guardianship, lest the legislative violate the basic law's provisions, is a third important feature of our constitutionalism, whereas the British have maintained for many years the "sovereignty of parliament." Thus, to mention only these five important points, the story of modern constitutionalism may in many ways be depicted as a great debate between American and British principles. And yet, in each of these points there also is contained a shared and common element, and in course of time American constitutionalism has developed in the direction of British as the British has developed in the direction of American conceptions. The British constitution has become more formalized [13] as the American has been overgrown with custom and judicial interpretation.[14] The American president has become increasingly dependent upon Congress, as the British prime minister has become increasingly independent of Parliament—both due to the paramount importance of the majoritarian party system. The American federal order has become more centralized, as the British Empire has been differentiated into the British Commonwealth of Nations, even if the United Kingdom has continued in a centralist direction. Even judicialism has been making headway in Britain, although no judicial challenge of legislation is admitted, while the Supreme Court has adopted "self-restraint."

It stands to reason that a set of concepts, principles, and propositions as flexible as the American Constitution has proved to be over the generations since its adoption cannot exert a uniform influence over so long a period as its almost two hundred years of existence. As was suggested at the outset of this introduction, its image was in successive ages shaped by interpreters who shared in the influence and impact of its basic concepts, principles, and propositions.

The Federalist, together with the great commentaries of Story and Kent,[15] was the decisive source for all those who would assess and possibly emulate the American example. Its strong conservatism and its lack of genuine sympathy for democracy readily persuaded men two generations later to turn to Tocqueville's *Democracy in America*. Although by no means ardently pro-democratic, the great French liberal displayed at least a tolerant determination to understand this decisive American thrust and while always on his guard —as were his numerous upper-class American friends and informants—he yet was willing to give the Jacksonian revolution the benefit of the doubt. Another two generations had to pass before the third great assessment of American politics, now become the long-established political order of one of the great powers, could rival its two preceding mirrors of American constitutionalism, James Bryce's justly famous *The American Commonwealth*.[16] More detailed and empirically elaborate, Bryce's portrayal sagely mingled much admiration and praise with sharp criticism and indeed at times condescension. It dominated the field and determined how men viewed the workings of our Constitution until the advent of modern American political science. This reborn special field of scientific inquiry has since provided friend and foe, native and foreigner, with such a plethora of highly specialized knowledge and sophisticated insight that it would have replaced the older portrayals entirely, were it not fraught with so many controversies and contradictions as to leave the constitution builder who seeks guidance in utter preplexity.

The very massiveness of scientific knowledge and the great variety of possible interpretations have served to blunt the impact and reduced the influence of American constitutionalism. This was the more so because of the ideological conflicts which have dominated the twentieth century and to which we have already alluded. Constitutional government and democracy, universally seen as the "wave of the future" until 1914, became, in the minds of many, relics of the past, a bourgeois past which was rapidly being superseded by a proletarian world. Only a few insisted that the basic conceptions of constitutionalism were as applicable to a workers' community as to a bourgeois one. My own work on this topic[17] was greeted by many progressives with more than a little doubt and scepticism.

It is only in the second half of the century—now that totalitarianism seems to have manifested its limitations, if it has not run its course—that the forces of reconstruction have turned to constitutional democracy as probably the least objectionable of the available forms of government. How this turn of thought has affected the impact of American constitutionalism in recent years will be part of what we hope to analyze in the chapters that follow.

CHAPTER II

PRESIDENTIALISM

Of the American president, Harold Laski has said that he is "both more and less than a king; both more and less than a prime minister." [1] There can be little question that the original conception of the American presidency was worked out by the makers of the American Constitution as a republican substitute to the hereditary monarch of English eighteenth-century constitutionalism especially as represented by colonial governors, but with the image of George Washington in their minds as the kind of man who could and would occupy the office. Yet, he was definitely to be more restrained than was a king. Alexander Hamilton took considerable pains in comparing and contrasting the two offices. His views are summed up in the belief that anyone who thought that the president had anywhere near the power of the British king was quite wrong. "There is no pretense," he wrote, "for the parallel which has been attempted between him and the king." [2] Since that time, monarchs have largely passed into the limbo of bygone institutions, while the American president has become seemingly the most powerful officer of a constitutional regime. Yet it has been argued in recent years that much of his apparent power is deceptive, and that his responsibilities greatly exceed his resources for fulfilling them. [3] This argument is only one part of an ongoing debate as to the "real" position of the American president in twentieth-century America. The pomp and circumstance of the office are assuredly imposing. It would be a serious error to discuss the impact of the American Constitution's conception of the executive establishment in the light of present-day practice, whatever it might be.

It is not our task here to provide a history of the presidential office; this has been done by a number of competent historians and political scientists.[4] Rather it is our purpose here to analyze the way in which its image has affected constitution-makers in other lands. Since most of these men were jurists, it stands to reason that the provisions of the Constitution and the discussion of them in *The Federalist* have played a decisive role. The president's role as party leader has played a minor part only, though its clear recognition by Bryce influenced such men as Hugo Preuss in their views.[5] Not infrequently the decisive limitation, provided by the Supreme Court and the federal system (see Chapters II and III), has been overlooked. Indeed, it is part of the perversion which accompanies the adaptation of American constitutional ideas in foreign lands that where one of the major institutions of American constitutionalism, such as the presidency, has been reproduced, federalism and judicial protection of human rights have not been. Thus Switzerland in 1848 adopted a federal system influenced by American ideas (Chapter II) while some of the Latin American countries adopted the presidential system without federalism, as did, at least to some extent, France under de Gaulle. The judicial protection of human rights and, more especially, the judicial review of legislative acts have found favor only in recent years, but they have done so in countries like Italy and the Federal Republic of Germany which decisively rejected the presidential system. It is curious, as we noted in the introduction, that the unsatisfactory experiences encountered with allowing constitutional ideas to have a piece-meal impact have never so far persuaded anyone to adopt them in their integral totality. There may, of course, be serious objections from the point of view of history, tradition, and social structure, but such considerations apply with almost equal force to the adaptation of particular features.

It is a decisive feature of the American presidency that its conception is closely associated with the constitutional idea of a separation of powers as an essential condition of free government, that is to say a government under law. To put it another way, a primary consideration in working out the presidency was to prevent it from becoming a despotic or tyrannical office in the sense of concentrating arbitrary power in the hands of the man occupying it. However the actual separation is worked out—and there were considerable differences among Locke, Montesquieu and John Adams or William Blackstone—there is always present the notion that power must not be concentrated. Even in Britain, which is often cited by those who object to the doctrine, the judicial power is firmly separated from the executive (as it was not in Locke's thought), and the alternation of parties provides a dynamic separation symbolized in the conception of "His/Her Majesty's Loyal Opposition." [6]

The makers of the Constitution were much concerned with the problem of how to make the president strong within a clearly delimited sphere. They wished to remove him from partisan politics as manifest in representative assemblies and to protect him from the "gusts of popular passion." This preoccupation found its expression in the thought given to his election and more particularly the electoral college. The Federalist is very enthusiastic about it as insuring the independence of the president. The party had, of course, not yet emerged as the mainstay of popular government. That is perhaps in part the reason that nine-teenth-century constitution-makers in countries, such as the Latin American ones and Germany, where parties had then become recognized, and were indeed the carriers of the constitutionalist ideology, did not undertake to adopt the electoral college. They were rather inclined toward popular election of one kind or another. And of course in the United States what remains of the electoral college is a mode of electing the president by majorities in the states, rather than by a majority of the national electorate—a residue properly forming part of American federalism.

The presidential system is one of four models of constitutional democracy, the other three being the cabinet system (Britain), the assembly system (French Third Republic), and the council system (Switzerland). Each has found some imitators, but the second and third more than the first and fourth. The Swiss council system has recommended itself only to very small states without much foreign-policy involvement (Hamburg, Bremen, Berlin, Uruguay), the American one primarily to Latin American states and more recently to de Gaulle. (The prime drafter of the constitution of the Fifth Republic, Michel Debré, preferred the British system,[7] which de Gaulle has perverted by widening the presidential powers until they formally exceed those of the American president, being less limited by the representative assembly, and not at all by either federal or judicially enforced constitutional restraints.) It behooves us, therefore, to ask why the American presidential system did not appeal to constitution-makers until the recent past, and why it may do so to a greater extent in the future.

In recent years the main argument has been in terms of the danger of the presidential office being transformed into a dictatorship, though not necessarily a totalitarian one.[8] This line of reasoning was especially common in Germany after the experience with Hitler.

Probably the most important lesson of the Weimar constitution's failure was a recognition of the danger of a dualism between a popularly elected (plebiscitary) president and a chancellor and cabinet responsible to popularly elected parliament. This lesson was an important argument against a proposal to introduce the presidential system. This proposal was made by two deputies, Becker and Dehler, in the main committee (Hauptausschuss) of the Parliamentary Council on January 7, 1949. The argument was a powerful one, and its proponents were clearly inspired by the paradigm of the American presidency. They questioned the wisdom of introducing a "nineteenth-century" system, namely the system of parliamentary government on the French model, with a weak and parliamentarily elected president, and pleaded for a "strong democracy." In order to have a strong and stable government, it would be best to have a chief executive who would be elected for a fixed term; the danger of his becoming a dictator they denied, since the legislative power would be clearly in the hands of the parliament.[9] Two SPD deputies, Carlo Schmid and Rudolf Katz, in extended analysis, rejected this proposal. In the course of their argument, they more particularly criticized the American presidency.[10] All in all, it is fair to say that "no high public office in the Federal Republic has been given its new form under such a profound influence of recent historical experience as that of the head of State, the Federal President." [11] The same writer adds that the appointment of Hitler was seen as the crucial discretionary act of too powerful a president. The argument could have run just the other way: a really powerful president as chief executive—not Hindenburg but, e.g., Bruening—would never have had any occasion to appoint Hitler, the defeated candidate, to the chancellor's office. But in spite of Germany's long monarchical tradition, or perhaps because of it, those most influential in establishing the federal constitution did not see it this way. In a sense, they had never grasped the true spirit of the American presidential system.

Similarly, it has been authoritatively stated that in Italy, where American conditions do not exist, the presidential system might easily have been abused and the presidential powers turned into a "dangerous and objectionable dictatorship." * [12] It is noteworthy that here again "American conditions" are cited without any indication as to what precisely in the American setting is so radically at variance with Italian needs and requirements. More particularly, the European constitutional architects seem rarely to have considered the gubernatorial system of the several states as a proper analogue of the presidential system, although as a matter of historical fact, already mentioned, the presidential office was in part fashioned in the light of American experience with colonial governors, which links it with the monarchical tradition from which the governor's office stemmed.[13]

What is probably more important is that the traditional notions of the American presidency, as expounded in *The Federalist* and in the constitutional debates,[14] linked as they are to the eighteenth-century ideas on separation of powers, do not appeal to twentieth-century politicians, accustomed, many of them, to think in terms of a "party state." They seem generally not to take into account the extent to which the American president as party leader is today "responsible" in a more modern sense. Traditionally, governmental responsibility is seen primarily as personal responsibility.[15] What the people want is treated as the measuring rod for the activities of those responsible to them regardless of whether such activities correspond to technical requirements or not. This outlook is based upon too rational an image of

---

* Unless otherwise noted, translations throughout this work are by the author.

the electorate. Even a responsible electorate is, especially in such fields as foreign and defense affairs, unaware of what their objectives, such as peace and security, call for in the way of detailed measures. A good deal of the success of such men as Adenauer and de Gaulle[16] is due to the fact that they perceived their responsibility in such existential terms. Formal provisions for the older "personal reponsibility" are ineffective as against this trend.

It is due to this constellation that "Konrad Adenauer soon became the pivot in the developing political system of the Federal Republic." [17] This was quite in keeping with the notion of responsibility expounded in *The Federalist* and seen as the core of the presidential system. The office, Hamilton had pointed out, possessed not only energy, unity, duration, and competent powers, but it was also made duly dependent upon the people, that is to say there was "due responsibility." [18] There can be no question that by the president's programmatic commitment and his need of popular support for reelection, he is made broadly responsible to "the people." This responsibility is reinforced by the fact that the opposition party is continually seeking to find fault with his every move. Furthermore, this broad responsibility is reinforced by an ever-widening responsibility to the Congress, not merely to execute the laws, but to provide policy guidance. If the constitution of the Federal Republic provides that "the Chancellor shall determine the guidelines of public policy," (Art. 65) it spells out what has in fact become the function of the American chief executive. Such a concentration of political power is the more striking, since it is embedded in a continuing system of formal divisions and fragmentation. Indeed, one could say that the Germans rejected the presidential system in theory, but accepted it in practice, though not entirely.

Thus it has come to pass that the presidential system,

although explicitly rejected by the constitution-makers of Bonn, has cast its shadow over the constitutional evolution of the basic law. Its crypto-presidential "chancellor's democracy" has in turn stimulated thought in France which has culminated in the presidential system fashioned by General de Gaulle out of what was intended to be a genuine parliamentary cabinet government of the British type. We cannot be sure just how much of a role American thought might have had, because the deliberations of the government and the "experts" are not a matter of public record, as is the case with constituent assemblies. It is never easy, even under the most favorable circumstances, to interpret a constitutional text as the product of the thought of its makers. When the record is not known, it becomes almost impossible. But whatever the "intention" of its makers, the changes which de Gaulle has brought about have made out of it a presidential system that contains a much more serious danger of dictatorial perversion than the American one, because of the weak position of the representative assemblies. As we said some years ago "there can be little question that the constitution was 'tailored' to fit de Gaulle as President." [19] The question we then added, namely "what will become of it once the man for whom the presidency was intended, disappears?" still is a valid one and speculation is rife on the subject. But then the image of General Washington was assuredly in the minds of many of the constitution-makers at Philadelphia.[20] Whether things will work out as well in France, or whether the situation will become chaotic when de Gaulle is no longer president is anyone's guess. It seems, however, the best considered view that France will not return to its former ways, but will continue in the path of strong executive leadership. The constitution itself certainly places the president at the head of governmental operations.

There had been a good deal of discussion in France during the preceding thirty years concerning the presidential system. André Tardieu in a much discussed book, *La Révolution à Refaire,* sounded a call for a vigorous executive, with explicit reference to the United States experience. There have been many voices raised which stated comparable views, especially since de Gaulle himself several times, notably in a celebrated speech at Bayeux in 1946,[21] took a similar position. So did Michel Debré in his writings criticizing the Fourth Republic. In *La Republique et son Pouvoir* he definitely expresses a preference for the presidential system which he sees exemplified in the United States. The key problem is what he calls "authority"; *autorité* seems to him best exercised by one—an ancient view going back at least as far as Homer. Even so, its institutional application to the requirements of modern political order and an advanced industrial system is another matter.[22]

But though the American experience may have served as an inspiration, the system established by the constitution of the Fifth Republic is decidedly not very much like the American presidential system. Many Europeans who are inclined to see a closer analogy overlook the American federal context within which it is placed. They also tend to forget that in spite of the party system the presidential office is definitely embedded in a system of sharply separated powers. Indeed, the federal system itself constitutes a reinforcement of the functional by a territorial separation. That was recognized by one of the fathers of the constitution of the Federal Republic[23] and is crucially important in devising a system of limitations for a presidential system that is not to be perverted into a dictatorship. For a highly centralized system, like the French, a presidential system raises problems therefore which are quite alien to the American presidency. But far from reinforcing the position of an independent legislature, the drafters, and more especially Debré, guided by the British precedent to some extent, undertook to combine the presidential with a cabinet government. This is not the place to elaborate further on the French Fifth Republic and its problems.

In the nineteenth century, the fact that the American presidential executive formed part of a separation of powers scheme was more widely appreciated. This was at least in part due to the fact that continental Europeans were still engaged in limiting the executive role of traditional monarchies which had exhibited a characteristic separation of powers of their own.[24] The ill-fated constitution of Germany, resulting from the revolution of 1848, which went perhaps further than any other nineteenth-century European constitution in following the American model, even though retaining the monarchical chief executive, placed the ruler in the perspective of the American presidency. Time and again, the deputies spoke of the "instructive example of America which had been the model of the preparatory commission, and one could not, without damage, deviate from it." [25] One of the most brilliant pamphleteers, Count von der Goltz had traveled extensively in the United States. Being a conservative, he believed that although the institutions of the United States did not correspond as fully to its conditions as 40 or 60 years earlier, they still insured the progress and freedom of its population more perfectly than any other conceivable constitution. At the same time, he insisted that, against those who would simply adopt rather than adapt the American constitution, this constitution is not suited for any European country without very essential modifications.[26] As far as organization is concerned, the primary problem seemed to him to be that of how to adapt it to the monarchical principle, that is to say the principle of heredity. That apart, the American presidency provided an adequate model for the structuring of a system of separated powers.

In Latin America, there was considerably less readiness to accept the American model. Thus in Argentina, at the time of the adoption of their first constitution, after independence, in 1817 the British system of cabinet responsibility was adopted at the outset. It had already definitely been fixed by a law in 1815. Even so, the American model exercised a continuing influence and the position that it ought not to be overlooked was explicitly and at length argued in the late nineteenth century.[27] It is interesting that in this connection the development of the American presidency, as depicted by James Bryce, was explicitly cited to the effect that the American constitution-makers had failed to adopt the British system of cabinet government and modeled their presidency on their notion of the executive power of the king, because they did not and could not know this system; it had not yet become fully institutionalized and neither Blackstone nor other writers on British politics recognized the emergent practice; nor had Montesquieu, of course.[28] Argentine scholars have pointed out that the situation at the time of Argentina's becoming independent was quite different. By 1810 the British parliamentary cabinet system had become consolidated and was well-known. Hence the founders of the Argentine republic never conceived of an executive power independent of the legislature, such as existed in the United States. This held true also for the provinces, so that in fact the independent exercise of executive power became identified with tyranny and dictatorship. One scholar goes so far as to say "except in times of tyranny, the Argentine Republic has never surrendered the exercise of the executive power to the will of a single person." [29] Even so he recognized that the Argentinians, having adopted the British system, practiced it as if it were the American, and, from this, believed the "personal government" has resulted which is the source of all the evils.

There are other states, such as Bolivia, in which the independent executive was adopted at the outset, and definitely by way of following the American example. One authoritative writer attributes this to the fact that, in all the Americas, constitution-makers faced novel conditions—those of underdeveloped countries one would say today—for which there were few precedents and hence no models to follow. Hence "in place of a king only with difficulty limited by a semi-elective chamber and by a cabinet of his own choice, they created an elective official, temporary and responsible, assisted by a ministry nominated by himself and confirmed by the upper chamber." [30] But it was repeatedly noted that the original intention of the framers for the choosing of so powerful an official had been destroyed by the rise of the party system. This development, so it was argued, meant a perversion of the institution, and has had "terrible consequences both for the morals and the ability of the chief executives." [31] It meant that the president, instead of being the leader of a nation, became the leader and instrument of a party. Castigating patronage, this author insists that the intentions of the framers, as expounded in *The Federalist* 58, have been nullified and not a man of elevated character, but one who knows how to cultivate popularity, is likely to occupy the office. What this means is that there will be danger that the presidents become "tyrants" in the ancient Greek sense who, supported by the masses (*bajo pueblo*), defy the other authorities and achieve unlimited power—a danger which has now become a real concern of Americans. The discussion is cast in terms suggested by the spoils system, as described and criticized by James Bryce.[32] Incidentally the huge and rising costs of the presidential elections are noted. It is evident that such thoughts, while somewhat dated, have not lost all their poignancy in the present constellation.

It is not surprising that in view of such commentary we find springing up in Latin America, as in Europe, a recurrent albeit romantic appeal against all imitations and for the recovery of native wisdom. Thus a Latin American writer in the 1930's passionately pleaded for a return to the views of Simon Bolivar, against the "tragedy of constitutional imitation." [33]

This sort of sentiment was less pronounced in the nineteenth century, at least wherever rationalist liberalism was strong. Thus in Brazil, after the collapse of the constitutional monarchy in 1889, the republican leadership was looking toward the United States for guidance.[34] Federalism (see following chapter) as well as presidentialism were readily taken over. The constitution of February 24, 1891, was based on a draft which was largely the work of Ruy Barbosa, "a close student of the constitution of the United States." [35] He did not hesitate to pattern the constitution of Brazil upon the American model, and more particularly to adopt the presidential system, with a popularly elected president directly responsible to the people, and able to choose his associates (ministers) freely and independently. But the powers of the federal government being inferior to those provided by the American Constitution, the president increasingly relied upon his emergency powers (power of intervention, Art. 6) to intervene in a state whose political behavior he disapproved of. He likewise felt compelled to abuse the state of siege (Art. 48) with consequent impairment of constitutionally "guaranteed" rights and liberties (see following chapter). Generally speaking, and within the scope of federal powers, the Brazilian president's powers exceeded those of the American president.[36] The constitution itself to be sure was based upon the traditional scheme of a separation of powers, including such checks and balances as the presidential veto and the nonparticipation of cabinet members in the work of the representative assemblies. But with the help of the emergency powers, the president succeeded in securing an altogether predominant position. This predominance of the president achieved, as in other Latin American states, a fairly general consensus, in spite of the inherent dangers of *caudillismo*. As has been noted, the constitution remained formally in force for about forty years (until 1930), but it developed further and further away from the American model it started with and eventually was replaced by a dictatorship.[37]

It is perhaps illuminating to turn from these Latin American discussions back to two European writers on America and its presidential system, namely Alexis de Tocqueville and Robert von Mohl. They both exercised considerable influence and helped shape the image of the American presidency. Mohl, in his study on representative democracy,[38] is primarily concerned with the transformations that have occurred in the process of the democratization of the American Constitution. But he places his argument within context of the French revolution, which for a while, he says, produced a representative democracy, but no scientific work of lasting significance. He contrasts with this situation the American writings, more especially *The Federalist*, John Adams, and Calhoun, besides the great jurists such as Marshall, Story, and Kent, and then adds that "what finally Tocqueville, refined and imaginative, has thought and written about the necessary institutions of a democracy, its conditions and its consequences, belongs among the best that we have in the political sciences." [39] He at the same time argues that a penetrating analysis can be hoped for only from such "as have grown up in a representative democracy, and have taken an interest in its activities." For "experience heightens the discernment" and he who would analyze such a system must be "permeated with the spirit of its constitution." But Tocqueville, he thinks, is an exception. With this general caution about his own work, Mohl proceeds to discuss, *inter alia*, the American presidential system. The transfer of concentrated power to a single person may occur merely in an emergency; but in America it has been adopted "as an institution based upon careful consideration." As such, it raises very difficult questions. After some sage comments concerning the impossibility of combining a democracy with a monarchical head he concentrates upon the kind of chief executive who is elected at regular intervals. He stresses—and this is hardly surprising in light of the rise of the third Napoleon—the danger that such a man will, especially if he is a famous general, arrogate unto himself all political power. It makes little difference in such a case whether the man is chosen by the people at large or by a parliament. This perversion can occur quite gradually, and often takes the form of an usurpation of power by the military. (The poignancy of these observations is surely made manifest by the experience not only in France, but in Latin America and the newly observed tendencies in the developing countries.)[40] After then reviewing the several possible modes of election, the length of office, and the danger of stalemates, if the election is popular and hence independent of the representative assembly, Mohl summarizes that none of the possible solutions to the several problems produces a perfect order. He surmises that representative democracy presumably has a great future and will have great appeal to new nations.

He complements these more specifically institutional observations by an analysis of the consequences of democratization in America.[41] He believes that one of the important, yet also most difficult tasks of politics, is to combine the consistent development of the ruling principle of a political order with an institution that prevents the noxious application of this principle. He considers it inherent in the workings of power that those who are in possession of it incline to extend it beyond its desirable limits. To guarantee the peaceful coexistence of several principles is the highest statesmanship, but he insists that this is not a matter of a "mixed constitution" as has often been argued (following Aristotle), but that of erecting a barrier against the misuse and abuse of power; what results are limited, not mixed, forms of government. And representative democracy challenges our attention in this respect, because the likelihood of its rapid spread makes a system of effective checks on the exercise of power crucially important. It is evident from the entire tenor of what follows that Mohl is not only a close student of John Adams and John Calhoun, as well as other American constitutionalists, but he appreciates the dangers which a progressive democratization creates for the American constitutional conception, especially in the office of the president. He stresses that all the representatives of the people, those who legislate as well as those who administer, since they are elected and re-elected by the majority, depend for their careers upon this majority. Such an arrangement is apt to tempt them into violating the rights of the minorities in order to curry favor with the majority. This tendency is reinforced by the role of the press, which is likely to do the same, and hence in a representative democracy the danger of the abuse of power is very great. Like Hamilton and Madison, he is much concerned with the "gusts of popular passion," and seems to fear that there is no solid barrier that has yet been invented against them. He notes the moderation which characterized the founders of the American Republic, and exclaims that it would seem well-nigh impossible to secure the adoption of a constitution such as they fashioned. Noting the change from Washington and Hamilton to Jefferson, then Jackson and Pierce, he speaks of a populist temper that culminates in nullifiers and know-nothings.[42]

He believes that European statesmen have every reason to study the American developments most carefully, regretting the preoccupation of democratically inclined men with Rousseau and his doctrines. Noting the enormous progress of the United States, which had become "one of the most powerful countries" (1860!), and the widespread dissatisfaction with the failure of constitutional reforms in Europe, Mohl believes that many have turned to the United States as a panacea without knowing much about it. Hence it is of paramount importance to explore its inner workings realistically. That is made easy because of the extent to which all governmental affairs are publicized. "One moves in an open market," he exclaims. The most important observation is to recognize the steady progression of the democratic principle. The views of the founders on the score of the limits of popular wisdom have been abandoned, and barriers have been eliminated. He sharply criticizes the trend toward popular election of judges, and with positive horror he contemplates the day when all women will be allowed to vote.

In spite of these and other serious flaws, Mohl is convinced that the power of the United States will continue to increase, although he fears that if it does the tendency will become stronger that unjust and antisocial instincts of the masses will prevail.[43] He shows small appreciation for the regenerative powers of a democratic society, and seems to believe that the trend downward in the quality of presidents will continue—in the very year in which the greatest of American presidents was elected, Abraham Lincoln. Not exactly antidemocratic, but rather opposed to the utopian expectations which many European democrats entertained, he excuses himself for not proposing any remedies. He seems curiously unaware of the barrier which the Supreme Court had developed into over the years, and hardly mentions the possibility of a conservative party as a genuine barrier to excessively rapid change. A quick glance at the presidents who have served during the century since Mohl wrote suggests that conservative and progressive chief executives have fairly regularly alternated, both on the national and the state levels, and that even the markedly progressive ones, like Wilson and Roosevelt in this century, have been rather conservative at heart, and that on the whole the very workings of the electoral system produce middle-of-the-roaders rather than radicals.

Mohl's analysis is that of the liberal bourgeois. It resembles the much more famous study of Alexis de Tocqueville. In his *Democracy in America,* written a generation earlier, the distinguished French political writer (and practitioner) had struck several of the notes we have just indicated, without the benefit of the experience of the intervening years. It is well known that the tyranny of the majority is a central theme of his analysis; it worried him, too. And this in spite of the fact that he, as has been pointed out,[44] does not give a single instance of such "tyranny." It was, of course, common talk among the upper-class Americans among whom Tocqueville moved during his sojourn.

As far as the presidency is concerned, Tocqueville had dealt with it at some length, contrasting it with the constitutional monarchies of continental Europe.[45] After describing the constitutional provisions, he gives vent to the old-fashioned notion that the legislature is in the nature of things the stronger arm, which is apt to arrogate to itself the discretionary power which the executive ought to possess—a state of affairs which a generation later seemed fast in the making in the latter days of the powerful speakers, notably Reed and Cannon, and which precipitated Woodrow Wilson's critical study.[46] Tocqueville notes the limits which the federal system imposes, notably in contrast to France. Making legislation the hallmark of sovereignty, as had become traditional since Locke, if not Bodin, he argues that "the president is placed beside the legislature like an inferior and dependent power." To those who have in this century witnessed the steady rise of the presidential role in legislation and policy making, this argument seems far off the mark. It is due no doubt to Tocqueville's failure to assess the role of the parties realistically, and therefore to perceive the possibilities inherent in the president's function as leader of the majority party. He dwells on such points as the number of officials the president might appoint—a mere 12,000 as contrasted with the French king's 138,000. To Tocqueville the absence of foreign threats and relations leaves the president with less power than he might have otherwise. "In all his important acts he is directly or indirectly subject to the legislature, and of his own free authority he can do but little." And that is the reason, Tocqueville argues, he does not need a majority in the two houses; it is his weakness rather than his strength which explains it. A similar reflection is offered concerning his election: "to attempt to render the representative of the state a powerful sovereign, and at the same time elective, is, in my opinion, to entertain two incompatible designs," he thinks. No passion is being aroused over the president's election, because "he has but little power, little wealth, and little glory to share among his friends,"—and that in the days of President Jackson!

Tocqueville's assessment of the elections is as unrealistic and misleading as is his view of the presidency. He spends much time arguing that, only because the chief executive is weak, does his being elected work. Filled with a settled prejudice against elective heads of state (he twice refers to the case of feudal Poland!), he stresses the "corruption" which an electoral system involves, then praises the makers of the Constitution for providing the electoral college, which he describes at length and quite unrealistically. By the mid-1830's it was common knowledge that the electoral college had become an ineffectual appendix, due to the workings of the party system; yet Tocqueville writes as if it were an operating body of great significance. In this connection, he is particularly concerned with the dispatch which its mode of procedure allows, yet recognizes that it failed to agree in two cases, which Congress had to decide. Writing with a background of the monarchical tradition of France and other continental countries, Tocqueville stresses that it is "one of the principal vices of the elective system" that it produces instability or what is often spoken of as discontinuity in domestic and foreign policies. Again, he thinks that this "evil" is reduced when "the power vested in the elected magistrate is small." This is a problem which it would take much space to deal with adequately.[47] Certain it is that such a view springs from a basic lack of sympathy for party democracy; for what is the sense of it, if the parties do not represent genuine alternatives of domestic policy. As far as foreign policy is concerned, the American presidential system has over the years managed to produce a considerable amount of continuity, through such devices as bipartisanship; anyway, the parties are not divided according to foreign policy whose issues run through both parties.[48] But Tocqueville's view that the problem is not serious, because "the policy of the Americans in relation to the whole world is exceedingly simple," if ever true, certainly does not hold today. His argument is based on the untenable position (in the light of experience) that "the more precarious and the more perilous the position of a people, the more absolute is the want of a fixed and consistent external policy, and the more dangerous does the system of electing the chief magistrate become." [49] The capacity of an electorate organized in responsible parties to cope with this problem has proved much greater than Tocqueville and his contemporaries expected, and the apprehension that "few nations of Europe could escape the calamities of anarchy and conquest every time they might have to elect a new sovereign," meaning a chief executive and head of state, has proved quite groundless. Yet, the views of Tocqueville, as here sketched, exerted a profound influence[50] and are no doubt in considerable part responsible for the reluctance of constitution-makers to adopt the presidential system and to stick rather to a republicanized version of the British parliamentary scheme or what was believed to be such a scheme.

It might be worthwhile to note here another point on which the great Tocqueville entertained quite fallacious notions; that was the question of re-election. "The principle of re-eligibility," he wrote, "renders the corrupting influence of elective government still more extensive and pernicious." He thought that it "directly injures the very source of national existence," [51] because the president will deflect all his interest to being re-elected. In this connection Tocqueville stated the seemingly "realistic" but actually incorrect notion that it is "the chief aim" of any president to be re-elected. For while this undoubtedly is a motivation, it may well contribute to his seeking to discover the right course of action, rather than deflect him from it. Generally speaking, constitution-makers in Europe and elsewhere paid little heed to this particular concern of Tocqueville, but provided for the possibility of re-election.

The influence of Tocqueville generally declined in the second half of the nineteenth century. He was superseded by the end of the century by James Bryce. Being a Britisher and fully alert to the workings of parliamentary government, his reassessment of the presidential system and its setting within the living American constitutional order had of course a particular value for all those who tried to determine the relative values of each. It would be interesting, but unfortunately would lead too far afield, to explore critically Lord Bryce's sophisticated treatment of the American presidency at the turn of the century. There can be no question that his views shaped the views and attitudes of constitution-makers at the end of World War I and even World War II.[52] He helped to shape the general attitude in the third period, when it was generally felt that America was so rich, so powerful, and so vast that political institutions well suited to the management of so unique a governmental enterprise were almost by definition out of the question for a national state of limited dimension.

In the debate in the German Parliamentary Council to which reference was made earlier, the German scholar-politician Carlo Schmid put this well when he said in rejecting a proposal to combine the positions of president and chancellor as in the United States: "Such a vast power seduces men into abusing it; and power can be too easily misused, if the head of state who at the same time is chief executive who cannot be overthrown has at his disposal a well-integrated civil service trained to order and command."[53] Professor Schmid thought such a civil service or bureaucracy to be at the disposal of an all-powerful president in Germany. Many Americans would urge today that the rise of a sizable bureaucracy has produced comparable dangers in the United States.[54] Still others, among them myself, would rather be inclined to consider it possible to render such a bureaucracy responsible and thereby restrain the abuse of presidential power.[55]

At the same time, it is precisely the need for vigorous and if necessary decisive action, unhampered by the need to consider parliamentary majorities, which has made constitution-makers in recent years look with increasing interest at the American presidency as a paradigm of how to organize effective executive government. Especially in the newly developing countries, in Africa and Asia, the efforts of British advisers to set up parliamentary systems have been crowned with anything but success, when their advice was accepted.[56] In one after another of these states, a shaky parliamentary democracy has been superseded by some kind of military rule, and it may well be questioned whether these countries would not have been better off with some properly modified presidential system.

It is in this connection not without interest that in the recent crisis in German parliamentary relations—a crisis that developed in spite and perhaps even because of the much praised system of making the nonconfidence vote depend upon the choice of a new chief executive (chancellor) —a call for the presidential system has been voiced. Such thoughts a leading editorial writer of *Die Welt* (Hamburg) expressed in commenting upon the recent re-enactment of the politics of parliamentarism: "It may be necessary to do what the fathers of the Basic Law—too much influenced by the fathers of Weimar—failed to do: namely a distribution of powers which would give us a constitutional democracy rather than the absolute rule of a parliament. After the storm of the last few months, all ought to recognize: forms are not sacred. What is decisive is that a democracy remains effective even in this changed world of an industrial society." [57]

CHAPTER III

FEDERALISM

Of all the features of American constitutionalism, federalism has had the most decided impact abroad. Indeed, so far flung has its impact become in recent years that it is well-nigh impossible to trace it even in outline. It is literally true to say that wherever federalism is discussed, the discussion is cast in terms of American constitutionalism. This is due not only to the novelty of the Constitution's provisions, but also to the vigor and penetration of the analysis embodied in *The Federalist*.[1]

It has even been claimed that federalism is an American invention.[2] While an overstatement, it can be defended, if the particular kind of union created in 1787 is taken as the paradigm of "genuine" federalism, as it often is.[3] For never before had so close a union been combined with so much freedom (or autonomy) of the component parts. Past attempts at federal union had usually remained at the level of a league or long-term alliance, and from the contrast between these loose confederations and the effective federal government, jurists developed the dichotomy of *Staatenbund* and *Bundesstaat* (a confederal union of states and a federal, united state) which has dominated and in a measure bedeviled the discussion of federalism in terms of the elusive and paradoxical concept of sovereignty, dear to political oratory.

The builders of the American Constitution were happily

43

unconcerned with so abstract an argument. Being able men of practical affairs, they saw the situation as it concretely confronted them. Since the first attempt at building a constitution, as embodied in the Articles of Confederation, had proved inadequate to some of the pressing policy problems of the time, they revamped the scheme. Men confronted with similar situations or what they believed to be such have drawn inspiration from the American plan, even as it evolved over the years, as all governmental systems must, and a federal system more particularly will.[4] With this process of evolution we shall not be concerned here, except incidentally. What must interest us are the efforts at adapting American federalism to specific constitutional situations, such as the Swiss situation in 1848 and 1878, the Latin American one throughout the nineteenth and into the twentieth centuries, the German reconstruction in 1919 and 1948/9, and the European unification in mid-century. But something more in the way of background needs to be said on the American principle itself.

Neither Plato nor Aristotle nor the many political writers following them developed a concept of federalism.[5] It emerged slowly out of vague beginnings in the Middle Ages and was given a first significant general formulation by Johannes Althusius in the early seventeenth century, but without receiving any significant further development; even Montesquieu, though influential in the thought of the American constitution-makers, did not explore the problems of a federal government. This happened only when the drafters of the American Constitution sat down at Philadelphia to hammer out their compromise, although the Articles of Confederation constituted a more significant beginning than is often recognized.[6]

It is no exaggeration to say that the question as to how to structure the union of American states, that is to say federalism, was the most central issue of the constitutional convention at Philadelphia.[7] The discussions over its various aspects fill many pages of the record as reconstructed by Max Farrand. To be sure, some of the issues taking the greatest amount of time, such as that of protecting the small states against the large, turned out eventually to have been quite unrelated to the realities of American politics. As soon as parties and interest groups became organized and operative, they rendered these issues unimportant; indeed eventually it became a question of how to avoid excessive influence of interests entrenched in small states.

The much maligned and little studied Articles of Confederation (1781) had made a significant beginning in initiating a new federalism. They went beyond the framework of earlier contractual federalism. For while insisting that the several states were retaining their "sovereignty, freedom and independence," they yet proceeded not only to set up a separate federal government, but to make a start in the direction of constitutional federalism under which this government is that of individuals. Yet on the whole the confederation was built on earlier principles. Montesquieu's great influence gave his vague ideas about the federative republic as a purely defensive mechanism wide currency; at the same time, it was Montesquieu's insistence upon the difficulty of maintaining a republican form of government over a large territory which stimulated the belief in the general idea of federalism. The governing functions attributed to the confederation were mainly defense, foreign policy, western lands, weights and measures, trade with the Indians, posts, currency, and credit. Even so, the Articles contained no mention of a federal executive. No direct taxing power was provided for the confederation. In short, it was a confederal scheme feebler than the Community of the Six, and quite in line with what General de Gaulle would readily accept, except that he would of course have no use for the Congress which provided the keystone to the arch of this institutional structure.

So loosely constructed a federalism could not hope to deal effectively with the tasks confronting the emergent nation; economic crisis, political confusion, and foreign threats pushed the United States toward a closer union. The ensuing argument was, however, not cast in terms of a discussion of principle, such as has so often characterized the constitutional debates on federalism among those who sought to emulate the Americans, but concentrated on the concrete failures in governmental operation and how they might be remedied. This is not the place to recount or even summarize the long drawn-out debate between the promoters of the "Virginia Plan" and those of the "New Jersey Plan," between centralizers and decentralizers, between the advocates of large states and small states. Suffice it to say that the new federalism emerged as a compromise between those who were prepared to give the national government limitless superiority and those who would keep the central government weak in order to protect the local autonomy of the component states. A middle group of unionists helped, with much careful attention to practical detail and little dogmatism, to work out a feasible compromise. This compromise embodied what was in fact an entirely new concept of the federal state, or better, of a federal political order. This order was composed of a strong presidential executive, a national representative legislature composed of two houses, one representing the nation and one the peoples of the several states, a judicial guardian of the Constitution, and, after the first ten amendments were passed, a broad guarantee of human rights and civil liberties; and last but not least a federally structured procedure for amendment, itself a novel device in the history of constitutionalism.[8] Clearly, the new order went way beyond a merely defensive union: it provided, and was meant to provide, a broad framework for a national economy and a progressive national being.

The debates at Philadelphia are very revealing concerning the new federal concept, even though the drafters were unconcerned with theoretical problems. They were preoccupied with problems such as how to divide legislative power between the states and the federal government, how to balance the fields of governmental activity so as to produce a stable equilibrium between states and nation, and finally, as mentioned, how to arrange matters so as not to favor either the large or the small states. The new concept of federalism rests upon the notion that in a federal system of government each citizen belongs to two communities, that of his state and that of the nation, that these two levels of community should be clearly distinguished and effectively provided each with its own governmental institutions, and that in the functioning of the government of the inclusive community the component units ought to play a distinctive role.[9]

It is evident that this new conception of federalism would have a great appeal wherever the task presented itself of combining unity with diversity. Such a task imposes itself whenever, in a given population, some values, interests, and beliefs are shared by most men (and women), but wherein there exist distinct and territorially circumscribed subgroups cherishing separate and reasonably different values, interests, and beliefs which may be complementary or supplementary to the common values, interests, and beliefs. Often, one can speak of a culture and its subcultures, though in newly emerging nations this way of putting the matter is somewhat unrealistic. In countries such as Switzerland and Germany, where the people at large had developed autonomous political orders of a local or regional kind, the new federal conception seemed to solve the problem of how to unite without losing the local identity. The same holds, of course, for a vast cultural entity like India; it also can be applied, *ceteris paribus,* to Europe. The thought of the so-called European Federalists is explicitly and admittedly inspired by the American conception.[10]

It should, however, be recognized that this new conception, highly dynamic as it turned out to be, does not apply only to situations in which hitherto separate states wish to unite and form a union government, but also to those others where a hitherto united state, presumably in autocratic form, is breaking up into older component units that may be anxious to preserve a measure of cohesion (Prussia, the British Commonwealth, or Nigeria, *e.g.*). The "federalizing process" may, in other words, work either centripetally or centrifugally, and federalism provides a rich variety of intermediary ways of organizing a political order in such a way that both unity and diversity are reasonably served. Indeed, in ongoing federal systems, there is generally to be observed a certain up and down of these two opposing tendencies. While there may be a secular trend in one direction or the other (United States versus British Commonwealth), the drama of federal politics is to a considerable extent mirrored in these oscillations of the federalizing process.

What has just been said is of course very germane to the American order. American federalism has undergone a considerable evolution, punctured by the revolutionary drama of the Civil War. Although fought to "preserve the Union," in Lincoln's favored phrase, the outcome of this war served to shift the balance decisively in favor of the national government. The formal signal and symbol was the adoption of the Thirteenth, Fourteenth, and Fifteenth amendments.

It has been authoritatively stated that "one constitutional fact concerning pre-Civil War United States is difficult to keep in mind a century later—the absence of the Thirteenth, Fourteenth, and Fifteenth amendments. Some of the then unhampered State powers are startling today." [11] As this observation suggests, then, it was not so much an increase in national power as it was a decrease in local autonomy that the Civil War wrought. The extension of national power was largely a consequence of the industrialization which followed upon the Civil War. Actually the American federal concept was not basically affected by these changes, and in any case exerted its most powerful influence in the form it was originally given by the framers, with one important qualification. The democratization which transformed American politics during the first half of the nineteenth century was taken for granted by its emulators. But the party system, which was its institutional expression, was not generally recognized as transforming the American concept, since the parties themselves appeared organized in the light of it. [12]

In order to discuss the impact of this set of principles—the American conception of federalism—upon political thinkers and actors abroad, it seems necessary to divide the story both as to time and place. First, we shall consider its role in the constitution-making of Switzerland in 1848 and Germany in 1848, the one a process of revamping an ancient order, the other an abortive attempt at setting up a new one. We might next consider the reception of American federalism in Latin America, more especially Argentina, Brazil, and Mexico. We should then turn to its role in structuring the German empire and what became the British Dominions of Canada and Australia. A new burst of influence occurred after World War I, with the American concept providing a measure of guidance to the makers of the Weimar Republic, but more dramatically failing to do so, when the American concept was projected outward as a paradigm of world organization by Woodrow Wilson. Curiously enough, the American federal idea at the same time helped to mold the Soviet constitution of 1919. Finally, after World War II, the American concept served as a corrective, though of limited efficacy, in the rebuilding of German federalism and in shaping the Indian Republic's new constitution.

It is obvious that so varied and variegated a pattern of impact and influence can only be highlighted by brief indications of what points came to the fore in the constitutional debates and a few influential writings of the period. In the case of Switzerland a number of vigorous minds had come to feel in the thirties of the last century that "the American system contains the only principle which can save us," as their perhaps most vigorous spokesman, James Fazy, exclaimed in defending the instructions to the Genevese delegation which he himself had written.[13] This principle is that of bicameralism of the type which the American federal Constitution had employed to provide representation for the two communities, the national and the local. It is interesting to see how this "principle," although clearly recognized by a number of publicists—not only Fazy, but also Thomas Bornhauser, E. P. V. Troxler, and A. K. L. Kasthofer[14]—did not at first appear in the discussion. Very much like the American convention, the Swiss constituents went about their task quite pragmatically, as they were at the outset confronted by a centralist plan, corresponding to the Virginia Plan but containing the proposal for a unicameral national legislature (proposed by some of the large cantons) and an opposed plan for continuing a federalistic single legislature (the diet of *Tagsatzung*, in which each canton was equally represented). The defender of both tradition and radical innovation often critically commented on the American plan as alien to Swiss unicameral practice. But as the two extremes battled each other, the partisans of bicameralism seized their chance since their principle provided a way out, a reconciliation of the two demands, one for national and the other for local representation. What this meant, of course, was that constitutional federalism was prevailing against contractual federalism. What worried the Swiss, though, as events proved unnecessarily, but in light of the facts understandably, was that Switzerland did not possess the kind of balancer which other bicameral systems could boast.

In the constitutional monarchies, such as Britain, the monarch could step in to settle sharp conflicts between the two houses, whereas in the United States the same could be done by the president, or so one thought. Actually the realities of the party system had already to a considerable extent carried American political practice beyond this sort of checking and balancing of which eighteenth-century thought had been so fond. The Swiss, in keeping with their radically democratic ways, eventually had the Swiss electorate at large, through plebiscitary (referendum) consultations, provide this balancer. The reference to American experience is, of course, not always favorable. Indeed, the advocates of bicameralism at times ran into vigorous antiforeign feelings which are quite common in Switzerland. Thus one of these "Switzerland for the Swiss" supporters declared: "The system of two chambers is a system borrowed from North America which adopted the bases of the English constitution, and it is [therefore] not at all appropriate to the totally different circumstances of the Swiss cantons." [15] In spite of such objections, and on the basis of a plan in which foreign example and native tradition had been skillfully blended into a bicameralism of complete equality of the two chambers,[16] the constitutional drafting commission recommended it unanimously. Its main advocate (from Geneva) pointed out that such a system "has the advantage of conserving the sovereignty of the cantons, to guarantee them the rights which are precious to them on account of their historic tradition and to make real the assurances which were given the small cantons," while at the same time giving the nation a chance to make itself heard.[17]

What had occurred in the committee, recurred in the Assembly. Again the precedent of the United States was frequently cited, both to support and to combat the bicameral federalism which the committee had proposed. It was more particularly urged that this system had no appeal to the Swiss, because they had always operated unicameral systems, and feared the conflict of two chambers. The summary of the most eminent Swiss commentator, Professor William E. Rappard, seems to put it well, when he wrote: "the committee and the diet carried out a masterstroke, when they provided the Confederation with a bicameral parliament. They succeeded in reconciling, by a transaction which turned out very happily, the irreconcilable logic of reason and history, of modern democracy and of tradition, of the large and the small cantons. This transaction . . . resembles very much the compromise realized in the United States a half century earlier. But if thus the American Congress appears as the prototype of the Federal Assembly, the Swiss parliament is by no means a servile imitation of its transatlantic model. Similar causes rather engendered the same effects in Philadelphia in 1787 and at Berne in 1848." [18]

Perhaps the most general influence of the American federal concept as of the presidential one in the thought of constitutional draftsmen, at least in Europe, is to be found in the German constitutional assembly which sat at Frankfurt in 1848. Dubbed derisively the "assembly of professors" it did indeed gather the most learned, if not the most experienced or practical-minded, of constitution-makers. Many of them were close students of the American experience, and the records are replete with references not only to the Constitution and *The Federalist,* but also to the leading commentators, Story, Kent, Tocqueville, and their own Mohl.[19] Unlike their Swiss colleagues, who are also continually referred to, the German draftsmen had to overcome two powerful objections to the American precedent: (1) that Germany would be composed of a union of monarchies, not of republics, and (2) that Germany was composed of adjoining unitary monarchical national states, which fact exposed her to dangers absent or at least much reduced in the case of the United States.[20] It is truly amazing that in spite of these objections, the American federal scheme provided so powerful a motivating factor in the Frankfurt assembly. In explaining their decisions for structuring the federal power as they did, the reporter for the committee explained that "he who is concerned with the true form of a federal state will gladly look at the United States." The reason is "that in that country the problem is solved of how to harmonize the power of a central government with the fullest beneficial development of the several states." Referring to the writings of Jefferson, Story, Kent, Rawle, and Serjeant, who have "so admirably discussed in their works the nature of the federal constitution in its details," he notes particularly that the lacunae, the risks of unclear provisions, the obstacles to effective implementation, have been explored and enable the constitution-maker to guard against the possible failures of a federal constitution. He feels that America provides the image of a country in which the several states compete with each other in their legislation and administration, one excelling in commerce, another in industry, a third in education. And yet, so the reporter adds, the careful statesman will avoid blind admiration, since simple imitation will create dangers, when the circumstances are different. Here too, America's distance from powerful external enemies and its being a federation of republics is mentioned as of primary importance.[21] It is interesting that the principle of reserved powers for the states, and delegated ones for the national government, is recited and commented upon in these terms: "The several states retain thereby their autonomy (*Selbststaendigkeit*) and they continue to possess all those sovereign rights which are not expressly delegated to the national authorities (*Reichsgewalt*)." [22] In many other details, such as the treaty-making power of the states, the concentration of credit and so forth, American precedent is cited in support of the particular provisions proposed by the drafting committee.[23] Seeking to defend, as had the authors of *The Federalist*, their new national power against objections from those who wished to defend the established states, they claimed that "a wide, wonderful field of legislative and administrative activity remains in the future for each German state. As in North America, besides the beneficial common policy of providing certain institutions and arrangements in each state, a particular legislation fosters the noblest competition among the states, while recognizing the particular interests and peculiarities of nature, so in the German states such competition can be taking place for the well-being of their inhabitants." [24] Thus, the distribution of powers (competencies) is itself modeled on the American example.

Unfortunately, this fine constitution was never put into operation. Perhaps its very Americanism must be considered part of its failure. Yet, it deserves to be treated when one deals with the impact of American federalism, not only for its own sake, but because it served as a paradigm to later generations of Germans and indeed other Europeans. Not only the men of 1871, but also those of 1919 and 1949, remembered the reasoning and to some extent followed the lessons which this learned body of ardent constitutionalists took over from America.[25]

Throughout the nineteenth century, Latin American political leaders were tempted to follow the example of the United States in structuring their order in a federal way. They did not have to deal with the objections which met similar protagonists of American federalism in Europe. For neither monarchical governments nor ancient cantons, neither foreign threats nor distinct cultural traditions, divided Latin American states from the great exemplar of a federal order to the North. There was widespread feeling that federalism was the natural order for a civilized government.[26] Usually, the larger states, such as Argentina, Brazil, and Mexico, had been composed of provinces under Spanish rule, and these provinces had developed a certain life of their own. With distances great and government difficult to organize, federalism offered a ready republican solution. In Argentina, e.g., the provinces did not, as had the colonies in North America, develop legislative assemblies of their own which might have continued after the country's independence was won. Rather they were governed autocratically, and their first concern was to develop representative assemblies. This evolution occurred around the governor and legislative assemblies developed during the period of "anarchy and despotism" from 1820 to 1852, when the country's constitution was adopted and based on a federal pattern.[27] This federal pattern emerges quite definitely from the interaction of centralizing and decentralizing tendencies without necessary reference to the North American precedent.[28] In a study especially devoted to exploring the influence of American constitutionalism alongside that of the Spanish political tradition, T. E. Obregón many years ago noted (after citing *The Federalist* and Bryce) that the Senate, by combining the local and the national viewpoints constitutes the masterpiece of the American Constitution.[29] There was so general a disposition to admire the freedom and power of the *Angloamericanos* that federalism on the American pattern appeared a highly desirable institutional device for developing a similar political situation in Latin America.[30] But voices of sharp criticism likewise frequently were heard. Thus Obregón remarked pointedly that "one cannot give a better example of how little our legislators respect Mexican traditions than their having declared Mexico a federal republic." After pointing out that the United States was formed out of separate and independent entities, he said federating them meant giving them the form of a "united and strong nation," whereas in Mexico to make a federation out of a united nation was a fatal step leading to disunion.[31]

Such arguments from tradition and established usage are of limited value. Brazil, which had been governed monarchically in a unitary way for much of the nineteenth century, achieved a federal system of government in the course of the revolution which supplanted this government in 1890. The constitution of 1891 was a strongly federalistic one, explicitly modeled on, and yet in some respects different from, the North American pattern. The Brazilian case is one of federalizing a unitary state (precisely what the previously cited author denounced) and thus "the federal government was not only not the work of the individual states," but rather "these latter enjoyed no constitutional status of any kind until after the definite organization and actual functioning of the federal government created by the constitution." [32] It would be leading too far afield to attempt a detailed analysis of the old Brazilian federal system; suffice it to say that it was deliberately argued in terms of the United States' precedents. Ruy Barbosa, its true author, was according to all accounts not only a close student of the American federal system, but "profoundly influenced by the North American example." [33] His *Commentarios* are replete with references to Bryce and other writers on the United States Constitution, and he often and quite frankly declares that it was the Brazilian's intention to reproduce the American scheme as nearly as conditions permitted. It is often claimed that the Brazilian constitution did not succeed in making adequate allowance for these conditions. More basically, it is objected that the introduction of federalism artificially divided the country. Against such critics, Karl Lowenstein rightly observed: "it is evident that, in condemning federalism and state powers, the [Vargas] regime desires to strike at liberalism and democracy which, under the republic, had made a lasting imprint on the popular mind." [34]

The Brazilian case is not the only one. Indeed it has been argued that it has been a general tendency in Latin America to invert the federalizing process. [35] It is claimed that its "natural" way is to coordinate an existing diversity, whereas in Latin America it has been employed to "diversify existing historical unities." Such critics overlook the patent fact that it is by no means the only function of federalism to unite existing plural entities, but also to provide that diversity which is an essential condition for the growth and maintenance of personal freedom. To speak of it as "dividing artificially" existing political entities is to misunderstand the reason which inspired Latin American Liberals in the nineteenth century to imitate North American federal institutions.

The tendency to copy American provisions, especially to adopt the American system of granting limited powers to the federal authorities and to leave to the states a general competency, may be noted not only in Argentina (see above), but in Mexico and Venezuela as well; the same may be said concerning the general structure of two chambers, one representing the states, and concerning a judicial body to settle disputes between national and local authorities.[36] These provisions were however weakened by grants of a broad right of intervention which have tended to undermine the functioning of these federal systems in fact, especially in the case of Brazil (see Chapter II). Such trends have been recognized as the inevitable consequence of modern needs; the possibilities which a cooperative federalism provides have rarely been appreciated.[37] The fact that Latin American constitutions have merely taken over the formal provisions, but not the rich implementation, of American federalism has led quite a few authors to say, as does professor Sanchez-Agestea of Madrid, that federalism is subject to a universal decline in esteem—except where it serves to incorporate pre-existent political communities into broader organizations. The record does not support such a generalization. On the contrary, as the democratization process goes forward, many dormant diversities become more pronounced and only federalism in its many forms can hope to cope with the resultant centrifugal tendencies (Belgium, Canada, India, Puerto Rico).

It is, however, true that modern federalism, constitutional federalism, spread as a solution to problems of national integration, where the component units were highly organized. The most patent, and at the same time the most perplexing example is, of course, provided by modern Germany. After the failure of the unification effort at Frankfurt, and the elimination of the largely non-German Hapsburg Empire, the federal union of the remaining German principalities was achieved under Prussian leadership in the sequel of the successful war against France in 1871. This war between two empires, while occasioned by what appear to have been pretexts, was caused basically by the issue of German unification.[38]

Because of the hegemonic position of Prussia, some students of federalism have hesitated to consider the German empire a federal order. Though understandable, such a view is neither in keeping with German self-understanding, nor with the actual facts. Indeed, in some respects the German empire was more truly federal in terms of former and current conceptions than many other federal systems, notably the Latin American ones just discussed. Nor was the impact of American federal ideas negligible. European observers had, of course, been deeply disturbed by the American Civil War. It constituted a massive breakdown of what in the first half of the nineteenth century had been considered a viable constitutional order. Nonetheless, in spite of the monarchical and other deviations from the American presuppositions, it was the central idea of a *Bundesstaat,* rather than a *Staatenbund* such as had existed in the past, which the German constitution-makers desired and managed to establish. As Professor Emerson was able to show in his magistral study, in which the chapter on federalism occupies a central place, it was only in conjunction with the founding of the empire that federalism was fully explored, and, as he we believe rightly put it, the elaborate arguments in the entire controversy over *Bundesstaat* and *Staatenbund,* the federal state versus a confederation of states, were "derived from American sources." [39] The supporters of the federal interpretation argued from *The Federalist* and Tocqueville, those of the confederal one, concentrated in Bavaria, from Calhoun and Jefferson. Emerson is unquestionably right in insisting that at the outset "it was with foreign weapons that these early conflicts were waged." It was however only a matter of time until the evolution of the German national community rendered the confederal idea obsolete and therefore gave the victory to orthodox American views on federal constitutionalism. We shall have occasion to return to this issue presently in connection with the Weimar Republic and its successor regime. But before we do, it is necessary to cast a brief glance at the British colonies.

The problems of federalism for Canada and the other colonies were raised in Lord Durham's famous Report of 1868.[40] It was natural that the political order of the great Republic to the south of Canada's border should appear to be both example and warning. With the Civil War just ended and Freeman's influential study published a few years since,[41] it is remarkable how deeply influenced by American experience the great English statesman's conception really was. The basic problem which had to be faced was, of course, whether federalism could be combined with a system of cabinet government responsible to parliament, or whether it required a stable chief executive such as the American president (see Chapter II). Many were sceptical, but the final decision was to attempt the former. It has been said that "the Fathers of Confederation were alternately attracted and repelled by American federalism; attracted by the grandeur of the general design, repelled by some of its details." [42] More particularly they decided to let the national government have the residual powers, to define explicitly those of the provinces, and to make their cabinets depend upon the confidence of the lower house, thereby inevitably weakening the senate. However, these provisions were in time rendered nugatory by the Privy Council, which until 1949 judicially interpreted the constitution. The residuary clause was treated with as little respect by the Privy Council, as was the corresponding one favoring the states in the United States. In times of peace, it has been said, the Dominion government has been denied any significant power under it.[43] The Canadians had, however, a very special problem to deal with which found no parallel in the American experience: that was how to arrange a federal system that would satisfy their French-speaking citizens. There had been rebellion just before Lord Durham came to Canada as governor general and recent developments suggest that a solution which provided a reasonably satisfactory basis for about a hundred years is now gravely imperiled.[44] The earlier union of 1841 had already been put into jeopardy by this conflict. The British North America Act, adopted by the British parliament in 1868, would, by providing genuine provincial autonomy, solve the problem. It did for several generations. The impact of American federalism was quite decisive, although the American system was not as closely followed as it afterward was in Australia. Yet, one of the key builders of the Canadian constitution, Sir John A. MacDonald, said in the parliamentary debates that the American system was "one of the most skillful works which human intelligence ever created."

The Australian federal scheme, responding to quite different social and economic conditions than those prevailing in Canada—no powerful neighboring economy, no cultural minority—was closely modeled upon the American one, as described and analyzed in the pages of James Bryce. As one of the draftsmen wrote to a Canadian friend: "We at once naturally and indeed inevitably turned to the precedents from the United States rather than your own." [45] And yet, the Australians, too, desired to have a parliamentary government, and this fact caused some misgivings about drawing upon the experience of nonparliamentary systems. "We have the American constitution, the Swiss constitution, and slabs of the Canadian constitution hurled at us from all sides *ad nauseam*," exclaimed one of the delegates to the constitutional convention at Sydney.[46]

The problem which the British dominions had solved was

to plague the drafters of the Weimar constitution, or rather, it should have been a central concern of theirs, since they were determined upon a parliamentary system of government. Actually the discussions in the Weimar constituent assembly disclose that there was much greater concern with the structuring of federalism, and more especially with the breaking up of Prussia, thereby creating a more balanced federal order than the Prussian hegemonial scheme had been. In this effort they were to prove anachronistic. For Prussia was throughout the history of the Weimar Republic governed by the coalition of progressive elements, and her government led by the able Prime Minister, Otto Braun, would unquestionably have provided much needed balancing support for Weimar's weak structure. The destructive forces which undermined the ill-fated first German republic's political order arose in other parts of Germany, notably Bavaria, and it was Thuringia which was to have the sad distinction of conferring German citizenship upon Adolf Hitler without which he could not legally have become chancellor. For so strong was the federal tradition in Germany that this decisive right of deciding who should qualify as a citizen remained a local prerogative until 1933.

But the real strength of German federalism was rooted in the tradition of delegated administration. This practice, alien to American federalism in theory and until recently in practice, consists in letting the component units execute most federal laws.[47] In order to render it feasible the states (*Laender*) are not represented in a senate-like upper house, but in a council composed of the chief executives of the *Laender* who however for most purposes let themselves be represented by their surbordinates, from cabinet ministers to expert officials.[48] Arguments in the constitutional assembly, directed toward altering this system, were of little avail. Hugo Preuss, the draftsman of the constitution, was a close student of American government and politics. In his *Denkschrift* explaining the general part of the constitution, he showed himself fully aware of the extent to which the federalism of the empire had been a façade hiding the Prussian hegemonical scheme. He pointed out that "the Federal Council secured Prussia the power" by its artificial construction and was, as the organ of this union of princes, the alternative to a "unitary and popular state resting upon the free self-determination of the entire nation." To accomplish the latter seemed to him the paramount task of the Weimar constituent assembly. He therefore explicitly rejected the idea that the German republic resulted from a union of its constituent democratic states. "Not the existence of these states . . . is the first and decisive [consideration] for the political *Lebensform* of the German people, but the existence of this German people . . . there exists only one German nation." [49] He regretted the ready establishment of local constitutions and saw them as a danger, thereby completely abandoning the American conception which he knew but considered obsolete. And yet he knew also that Germany by her traditions was predestined to some kind of federal order. What he insisted upon was that this order should not be based upon Prussian hegemony, nor indeed upon the artificial dynastic states which had been developed, but upon the true division of Germany into regional groupings of distinct tribal traditions: the Swabians, the Hessians, the Bavarians, the Saxons, and so on. American and Swiss influences combine here to reinforce the sociological and historical argument with the constitutional conviction that a federal system presupposes a reasonably persuasive equality of the component units. Differences there must be, but while the contrasts may be great, there should be sufficient intermediary units. [50] These, Preuss thought, should have the functions of intensive self-government, especially in the cultural field. He

63

did not succeed in persuading his colleagues; Prussia was not abolished, but federalized in turn. But as time went on, the general trend of the evolution confirmed his original conception; just before the collapse of the Weimar Republic, a federal reform in that direction was being debated.[51] However, in all these developments, the American impact was remote and diffuse.

Of much more universal significance, however, than the confused situation in Germany was the worldwide thrust of American constitutional federalism as a solution to the problem of war and peace. Woodrow Wilson, by espousing the League of Nations, sought to give the American "idea" global application. The failure of the League of Nations does not alter the fact that it was the first attempt to organize the world federally for the pursuit of its common values, interests, and beliefs. In a variety of fields, notably the liberation of colonial peoples through trusteeship, the League was a projection of the American concept. Immanuel Kant, in his immortal essay *On Eternal Peace*, inspired by the American and French revolutions, had first sought to delineate such a federal world order, explicitly contrasting it with a world state, which he feared would turn into a world despotism. But he had prophetically laid down one essential condition which the United States federal system had observed, but which the drafters of the League covenant neglected: the requirement of political homogeneity. Only a confederation of "republican," that is to say constitutional, governments can erect a viable federal system. By disregarding this key condition and including autocratic regimes, first the Japanese empire and fascist Italy, afterward the Soviet Union, the League, as the United Nations afterward, violated a primary condition for effectiveness of a working federal system, very much more important than the much argued confederal issue.[52]

64

Altogether, the specific conception worked out at Philadelphia is far from being realized in the United Nations. The notion of a veto power for any *one* of the members of the Security Council would have horrified the makers of the American Constitution, though it would have pleased John Calhoun, whose theory of concurrent majorities it, in a sense, embodies. Such a veto is an understandable protection in a league which contains politically heterogeneous regimes. To mention just one other crucial point: the failure to provide for direct citizenship in the world community, while understandable enough in the face of members such as the Soviet Union, negates a key feature of the American concept of federalism as above described. No genuine political community beyond the sovereign national state is in fact recognized.[53] There may yet be good and sufficient reasons for maintaining an organization such as the United Nations, but its radical deviations from the federal concept of American constitutionalism should be clearly recognized. Let us for a conclusion return to the situation after World War I.

A curious and in many ways startling point of impact of American federal notions is the Soviet Union. It is, of course, quite arguable whether one need to take the constitution of 1918 as anything but a façade, and we ourselves have been inclined that way. However, Soviet federalism has a certain importance, on account of the many and highly divergent nationalities.[54] Here, as in so many other spheres, ideology had to yield to practical necessity. To be sure, Marx had considered federalism a system of government that was meaningless except in a liberal bourgeois society; the hostility of Marxists toward the thought patterns underlying federalism is well known.[55] Surely the dictatorship of the proletariat was not going to be federally structured! And yet, so powerful were the legitimizing potentialities of constitutionalism and with it of federalism, that the Soviet constitution of 1918 adopted a scheme which on paper at least would seem to have been conceived under American influence. Indeed, not only did federation appear the solution to their problems inside the Soviet Union, it was further believed that "around revolutionary Russia will more and more be grouped individual, different federations of free nations," and that "the Soviet Republic will sooner or later be surrounded by daughter republics and sister republics, which, uniting, will lay the foundations for a federation first of Europe and then of the whole world." Professor Towster has, I think quite rightly, commented that "Lenin was apparently considerably influenced by Stalin, then Commissar of Nationalities, who saw the American and Swiss federations as historical evolutions 'from independent states—through confederation to federation, while in fact they became unitary states preserving only the forms of federalism'." [56] This surely was the path the Soviet Union was to take, although prior to the establishment of the United Nations the Soviet Union reasserted its confederal scheme to the point of claiming that such components as the Ukraine were "independent" states. The actual unity of the political order is, of course, secured by the Communist party, which far from exhibiting the loosely confederal structure of parties in genuinely federal systems, such as the United States, actually is strongly centralized and hierarchically controlled from Moscow. [57]

Since the 1920's, and to an increasing extent due to the development of contemporary political science, the impact of American constitutionalism in the field of federalism has been quite limited and restricted to particular aspects of it. One special, and highly complex, situation needs perhaps a few words and that is postwar Germany. The establishment or re-establishment of a federal system was a declared aim of the occupying powers, especially the United States. [58] Yet

66

it has been rightly observed that "there was no particular reason why the Germans should have to look to the occupying powers for the cue to return to their federal traditions." [59] As we have already seen, federalism had a long tradition and one closely interwoven with the American conception, though quite distinct from it. As an alternative to Hitler's radical centralism, federalism had an additional appeal to many Germans. Particular policy initiatives like the States' Council (Länderrat) set up under American auspices contributed to the widespread disposition of Americans and Germans to agree on the general desirability of a federal constitution for postwar Germany. But it was a question of what kind. Generally speaking, the American policy struck the middle road which a majority of Germans also were inclined to favor: not a loose confederation of the kind the French at that time wanted, nor a return to the pseudo-federalism of the Weimar Republic which the British preferred. With Prussia eliminated by Allied decree, the road was clear for a more balanced pattern of reasonably equal component units.[60] Even without a presidential system, the Germans could have adopted more or less the American federal design: two elected legislative chambers of which one would represent the nation and one the states, clear separation of national and local functions and powers, and so forth. But the German traditon proved too strong. After an extended debate, the idea of a senate was discarded in favor of a federal council coordinating the state executives; delegated administration was resumed and thus federal and local functions intertwined. It is in fact striking, in view of the widespread interest in American ideas, how sparse were the references to American federalism in the discussion of the preconstitutional convention at Herrenchiemsee.[61] And when these problems were discussed in the so-called "parliamentary council"—the German constitutional convention of 1948/9—one of the leading delegates, Dr. Suesterhenn, recalled, during the discussions on the federal setup, that a high official of the military government had informed them at the time of Herrenchiemsee that the suggestions about federalism in the proposals of the military governors[62] were no impositions upon the Germans, but had been included in the light of the fact that both major German parties had, in their drafts for a German constitution, adopted the federal principle.[63] If there was an "impact" of American ideas, it occurred spontaneously and through informal channels, as indeed most of them had become embodied in the German tradition since 1848.

Before concluding, the impact of American ideas of federalism in the world at large deserves at least brief mention. The drafters of the complex federal constitution of India were much concerned with American experience,[64] as were other emergent nations. But none more so than the Europeans. In fact, much of the debate over the suitable form of a European Union has been in terms reminiscent of those over the Confederation. For a decade or more after 1948, the main debate among those favoring the unification of Europe was over the issue of federalism versus confederalism. There was often a lack of appreciation of the profound differences between the task confronting a limited number of agrarian colonies in the preindustrial age and that with which the ancient European national states were faced. The rhetorics of united Europe operated very uncritically with such slogans as the United States of Europe and the like.[65] But as Paul-Henri Spaak said, on the memorable occasion of presenting the draft constitution for a European political community, the proposed constitution was "partly federal and partly confederal." In other words, the issue was an unreal one; what mattered was the compromise between the two—where to draw the line. It is noteworthy that in preparing the draft, not only American, but Australian, Canadian, German, and Swiss precedents were carefully considered.[66] Unfortunately, this proposal, linked as it was to the Defense Community Treaty, died with the latter. Thereafter, the more serious work, especially since the establishment of the European Coal and Steel Community, and afterward the Common Market (1958), has been carried forward without any considerable attention to American precedents,[67] by building a structure pragmatically in the light of the practical needs of effective economic cooperation.[68] Still, the dream of eventually creating a close union resembling the American federal system persists and continues to exert a measure of influence.[69]

In conclusion, we may say that federalism in its particular American form has exerted world-wide influence. The insistence upon an operating unitary core, representing the community at large, and the equally strong insistence upon a truly autonomous set of component units, embodying the plurality of distinctive subcommunities composing the inclusive communtiy, remains the model by which federalists of all kinds throughout the modern world have been, and are, united. In any case, it is clear that the small state and the small political community can only hope to survive in a world of ever-widening contacts and interests if federalism is recognized, not as a panacea, but as a useful instrumentality of good government. Therefore, the beneficial impact of American constitutionalism in this field of politics is beyond the peradventure of a doubt.

CHAPTER IV

THE JUDICIAL POWER
AND HUMAN RIGHTS

Presidentialism and federalism are clearly American innovations which are universally recognized as such. The same cannot, of course, be said of human rights.[1] Not only does the history of human rights go far back into the past, but the American Constitution did not, in its original form, even contain a bill of rights; they were added, as everyone knows, as amendments to the original document. Not all of them, to be sure. Such basic rights as *habeas corpus,* the right of a man to his physical freedom, unless properly and promptly indicted, or the right to a jury trial are embodied in the original document, as is the contract clause which protects basic property rights against certain infringements.[2] But even so, many of the most "fundamental" rights and freedoms, such as the freedom of religion, of speech, and assembly, were added only in the amendments, and it is said on the inspiration of the French Declaration of Rights of Man.[3] But such a view overlooks the fact that the men of 1787 deemed it sufficient that these rights were guaranteed in the several state constitutions (as had indeed been the case since the celebrated draft which John Locke prepared for the colony of Carolina, never implemented, since Roger Williams' effort at having religious toleration constitutionally guaranteed, and more especially since the Virginia Declaration of 1776).

73

To be sure, no less a scholar than the famous George Jellinek pointed out, on the basis of research both by himself and others, that the French Declaration was itself greatly influenced by the bills of rights contained in the American state constitutions of which several French translations had been published in the years immediately preceding the French revolution.[4] And none other than Lafayette has left us a statement to the effect that his original proposal for a bill of rights, made in the *Constituante* in July 1789, was modeled upon the American bills: "Les constitutions que se donnérent successivement les treize états, furent precedées de déclarations des droits, dont les principes devaient servir des regles aux representants du peuple, soit aux conventions, soit dans les autres exercices de leur pouvoirs. La Virginie était la première à produire une déclaration des droits proprement dite." [5]

A proposal in the convention to have a bill added was voted down on the ground that "the state declarations of rights are not repealed by this constitution; and being in force are sufficient." [6] In the eighty-fourth paper of *The Federalist*, Alexander Hamilton had argued that besides the popular basis of the government and the numerous rights contained in the Constitution, which he lists, "bills of rights, in the sense and to the extent that they are contended for, are not only unnecessary in the proposed Constitution, but would even be dangerous." Since the government was one of limited powers, limitations might provide, he thought, a "colorable pretext" for claiming powers which had not been granted, such as regulating the press. Moreover, he thought the Constitution itself constituted a bill of rights. In spite of the cogency of these arguments, the demand for such a bill became so strong that the Federalists during the campaign for certification committed themselves to adding one, and so the first Congress fashioned the plain and straightforward amendments; they contrasted sharply with some of the rhetorical bills which a number of state constitutions contained. And they provided, as Professor Rossiter has rightly insisted, much needed additional legitimacy.[7] Thus, the basic human rights are, in all but form, integral parts of American constitutionalism.

Here we should like to interrupt the argument in order to insert a brief note on the amending power itself. The first ten amendments of the American Constitution, so vital to its entire history, would have been impossible to introduce, had not the men of Philadelphia wisely invented a process for such amendments. These provisions have now become so much a matter of course that it is often forgotten how remarkable an innovation they constituted at the time. The French revolutionaries neglected to provide for it, as had the several Cromwellian constitutions, though such provisions turn up in some state constitutions, like that of Massachusetts.[8] To see the function of amending the Constitution as at once a distinct and necessary "power" was, of course, implicit in their entire undertaking. But it received remarkably little attention, considering its novelty, and more especially its eminently noteworthy elimination of the consent of Congress as the *necessary* condition for amendment. (The alternative has, as a matter of practice, not proved of practical importance.)

But continental European and other constitution-makers have failed to appreciate its significance, giving the right to the parliamentary legislature as part of its rule-making function. Canada, of course, had to ask formally for an act of the British parliament when an amendment was desired, but the real decision was made by the Canadian parliament when it resolved to ask for one. The Australians, on the other hand, worked out an amending procedure which they expected would make amendments easier than in the United

States, but that hope has been disappointed.[9] The Australian case is an exception. Generally speaking even in federal systems, where the effective participation of the component units is vital, the ordinary legislative process was in most countries deemed adequate for the purpose of changing a constitution. Much ink was wasted over the distinction between "rigid" and "flexible," rather than "stable" and "unstable," constitutions in terms of their process of amendment. The most unfortunate result of this failure to see constitutionally guaranteed rights as requiring adequate enforcement and protection was the Continental, and especially Weimar, practice of adding to the statement of a particular right the phrase "unless the law provides otherwise." [10] Only since World War II has a distinct amending power been recognized in many constitutions, often in explicit recognition of the American Constitution's impact.[11] And yet, only when the basic law is protected against easy alteration, does the notion of the constitutional guarantee of human rights make any sense. Hence the recognition of the need for such enforcement machinery rather than the idea of human rights as such makes the influence of American constitutionalism manifest, whereas the impact of the idea of rights as such is so closely and indistinguishably intertwined with the influence of the French Declaration that the most painstaking research would not be able to disentangle these skeins. Being the manifestations of one great tradition, they mutually reinforced each other in persuading men everywhere that some such bill of rights was an essential part of deliberate constitution-making.

It is, however, at this point, necessary to direct attention also to the fact that these rights did not remain unaltered even in the land of their first formulation. Indeed the more than a century and a half which have passed since their passage have seen these rights undergo a very significant transformation. Not that they have been abandoned, though some of them, like the right of private property, have been seriously restricted. But they have been enlarged and in a basic sense transformed. In the view of the drafters, it was a matter of shielding the citizen against the grasp of the new government. Inspired by the suspicion of all power, the rights were rights "against" or "from" the government. But as the divergencies in conceiving such rights became more and more manifest, it became increasingly clear also that such rights were not something absolute and unchangeable. Rights were generally understood as expressions of human preference, as historically and socially conditioned. And as the process of democratization went forward, *civil* liberties, that is to say the rights involved in participating *in* the government, came to the fore, while at the same time the task of protecting the individual against hostile majorities was increasingly recognized, especially in response to Tocqueville's study of the "tyranny of the majority" and John Stuart Mill's *On Liberty*.[12]

At the same time, the concern over the helplessness of the invidual in face of massive social forces, especially economic exploitation, generated an entirely new kind of "freedom," which was first epitomized in the "right to work." These new freedoms are rights of an economic and social kind which characteristically involve collective and more especially governmental effort; the freedom from want, *e.g.*, calls for such complex activities as over-all planning, and hence we are here confronted with rights *through* or *by way of* the government. American constitutionalism has been slow in following suit. As late as the 1950's, a congressional majority rejected a bill of such rights which the Puerto Ricans had included in their new constitution, believing that what the Congress had accepted, when it approved the Universal Declaration of Human Rights adopted by the United Nations, it could not very well refuse to its own fellow-citizens. But Congress did. It is therefore not possible to see American constitutionalism as the driving force in this development, even though quite a few of these newer rights have found a place in American state constitutions.[13] But when they were included in the constitutions adopted after World War II in Europe, Asia, and Africa, it was often in opposition to, rather than under the influence of, American constitutionalism.

Why then should one include this subject of human rights in our discussion of the impact of American constitutionalism? It is, to repeat, because the United States has from the beginning been insistent that a declaration of human rights is not worth the paper it is written on unless it is accompanied by suitable provisions for their enforcement. The grandiloquent declarations of the French revolutionaries went by the board precisely because they were just declarations. The same may be said of the bills contained in the Soviet Union's constitutions. The Americans by contrast from the beginning, even in their state constitutions, were deeply concerned with how to make any such rights "stick," whereas Europeans have, until very recently, been reluctant to recognize that there is a problem involved which cannot be solved by reference to a representative assembly, as the British tradition had it. The solution which the Americans suggested for this crucial problem is "judicial review." This principle might even, for brevity's sake, be called "judicialism." [14] Here, as in so many other matters, American constitutionalism, presidential, federal, and judicial, has its dialectic opposite in the English constitutional tradition, which is antipresidential, antifederal, and antijudicial. Judicialism derived in a way from the fecund if vague suggestions found in Montesquieu.

The makers of the American Constitution did not explicitly provide for the courts to review the constitutionality of legislative acts, but as Alexander Hamilton was to point out in *The Federalist* such a power is implicit in an independent judiciary. He argued that the provision against bills of attainder, *e.g.*, could "be preserved in practice no other way than through the medium of courts of justice, whose duty it must be to declare all acts contrary to the manifest tenor of the Constitution void." [15] He rejected, and Americans came to reject generally, the notion that this implied a "superiority" of the judiciary over the legislative power. It is not necessary, we are sure, to recount here the powerful argument which Hamilton set forth in support of this contention, nor the history of judicial review from the basic decision of Marshall to more recent ones.[16] Nor need we dwell, for our present purpose, upon the significant distinction between a judicial review by federal (national) courts of the acts of state legislative bodies, and one which affects the acts of the national legislature. The crucial issue, and the one on which the impact of American constitutionalism needs to be traced, is the general one we have just stated. Rejected by most Europeans until recent years, even though they admired federalism and other aspects of American constitutionalism, it has been making rapid headway in a number of countries since World War II, partly because the practices of totalitarian dictatorship have made manifest the uselessness of bills of rights, unless protected against the arbitrary violations by an all-powerful party manipulating *pro forma* a "parliamentary" majority. But of course approaches to such judicial review go further back.

It is none the less noteworthy that the Swiss did not, in 1848, adopt judicial review. This is in part attributable to the fact that the radicals who carried through the constitutional reform were rather suspicious of the judiciary and its conservative propensities. It must also be remembered that in countries with a civil law tradition the judiciary is not seen in the same role as in common law lands. This comparative proposition ought not, however, to be overdone, since Britain under the influence of the philosophical radicals and more especially Bentham and Austin has in spite of its common law tradition been inclined to see the judiciary as strictly subordinate to parliament. Ever since Bentham launched his virulent attack against Blackstone, this trend has become predominant in England and to some extent in the Dominions as well.[17] Thus both Britain and Switzerland, the two foremost champions of liberal democracy in Europe, seemed to argue against the American tradition of judicial protection of human rights. Nor did the issue arouse much general interest. Only isolated voices of jurists were raised in favor, such as Duguit's famous plea for the judicial cognizance of the original Declaration as part of French constitutional law and Fleiner's argument in favor of it as a check on radical democracy.[18] These voices remained crying in the wilderness of legislative positivism.

The hope of some of these Swiss critics that judicial review might be inserted into the constitution by constitutional amendment has not been fulfilled. The radically democratic Swiss tradition, with the frequent participation of the people through referendum and initiative has presumably forestalled it. In fact, the Swiss constitution is noteworthy in that its article 103 expressly forbids the Swiss judiciary to consider whether a law formally adopted by the Swiss representative bodies is in accordance with the constitution or not. Fleiner has stated that there are cases when the question of constitutionality was simply disregarded. And when one recalls how much the United States Congress is influenced in considering constitutionality of its legislation, anticipating possible Supreme Court action, one cannot be surprised.[19]

An interesting beginning in judicialism was made, however, in the Frankfurt assembly of 1848. As in so many other matters, so in this also the drafters of this constitution of a united, liberal, and democratic Germany were particularly ready to acknowledge the impact of American constitutional ideas. One of the members of the assembly, in accepting the provisions for a supreme court (Reichsgericht), stressed the fact that the United States Constitution guarantees the citizens' rights against legislation and urged his fellows to follow the United States in this as in so many other matters.[20] There were, of course, voices which opposed it, because they thought the princes would just abuse such judicial review for the defense of their monarchical position. But that view was overruled. In very explicit and strong terms, Professor Mittermaier of Heidelberg offered a paean of praise for the American institution. "What is considered the finest ornament of the American constitution?" he asked and he answered himself that it was the Supreme Court. Without it, the Constitution would never have been able to develop, for it is the court that fills the lacunae, clears up the uncertainties. "The Constitution owes its life, its strength, the certainty of its provisions in detail to the Supreme Court." He combated the notion, expressed by some, that the judges are not capable of dealing with public policies, with political life. "These judges are no leathery jurists!" he exclaimed. For if such men are rightly selected, and they are in the United States, they can make the most "wonderful" decisions; they deal with cases, not generalities, and they determine whether a given law is according to the Constitution. In this connection he cited again the work of Robert von Mohl on United States constitutional law which had altogether such a great influence on this assembly, as it had had on the Swiss. He argued that Mohl was very clear and explicit on judicial re-

81

view[21] and had highlighted it as a key institution of American constitutionalism. So Mittermaier concluded that the Germans ought to adopt it, and they did.[22] His final appeal is touching in its optimism: "Let us follow the example of the United States and we'll earn the most marvellous fruit. Give us this keystone for our constitution. It would make freedom secure . . . it would make German unity feasible." [23]

The empire, of course, discarded all that, and a timid new beginning toward judicial guardianship was made only under the Weimer Republic. To be sure, the makers of this constitution, like their American predecessors, had made no provision for the exercise of judicial power for the purpose of restraining the legislative activity of parliament. But the issue soon arose and courts began to claim, even though rather haltingly, the right of judicial review. The claim was weakened by the fact that the constitution of the Weimar Republic did not organize a separate constitutional amending power, but provided only for a "qualified" majority in support of such legislation as had the effect of amending the constitution. Hence it could be argued that with no separate amending power the discretion was entirely with the parliament itself. Nonetheless, the courts proceeded. It is difficult to determine whether we may discern here a certain impact of American constitutionalism; the writings in the field and on the subject certainly suggest it.[24]

Judicialism also achieved a certain vogue in Latin American countries, as a possible means of coping with the worst excesses of personal government, the notorious *personalismo*. Dr. Santos P. Amadeo has given a very good account of how judicialism worked in Argentina, when that country was, as the then president of the Pan American Union wrote in his foreword, "one of the progressive democracies on this continent." [25] Besides the important role which the judicial power was called upon to play in the development of the Argentine federal system, it was crucial also in protecting civil liberties. "An outstanding feature of the constitutional development of Argentina is that each of its constitutions has contained a bill of rights for the protection of the individual against governmental action," Amadeo wrote.[26] But not only that; the judiciary article of the Argentine constitution of 1853 is one of the most important among those provisions of the Argentine constitution which "were directly taken from or modeled on similar provisions in the constitution of the United States." [27] As a result, the Argentine Supreme Court has, in reference to the provisions modeled on the United States pattern, "followed the decisions of the United States Supreme Court . . . provided that those decisions seem reasonable." There are good theoretical and practical reasons for that, especially where implementing legislation has likewise been guided by United States precedent. "Many Argentine statutes have been patterned after legislation enacted in the United States for similar purposes." Statutes have from time to time been held unconstitutional and thus a marked approximation to judicialism as known in the United States has been achieved. It would lead too far afield to explore similar developments in other Latin American states; suffice it to say that the judicial protection of human rights had a considerable development in Latin America during the nineteenth century.

But the really significant push in the direction of judicial review with the intent of protecting human rights came after World War II. In Germany, Italy, and a number of other countries, constitutional courts were instituted to act as guardians of the constitution. Even the early liberal doctrine of the neutral power was mobilized in support of the new impetus to follow the American example. Although Germany had not fully accepted the doctrine of a distinct amending power, two provisions in the Basic Law constituted a near approximation to it. Article 79 makes it obligatory for parliament to amend the constitution specifically and expressly, in other words amendments may not just by implication be carried through in ordinary legislation; both houses of parliament have to act by two-thirds majorities. A number of such amendments have been made; but only one, about military service, affects the human rights of citizens. But what is really important is that in view of the predominance of the two major parties, these two thirds can be secured, as mentioned, only by working out a compromise between them; in short, a kind of national consensus has to be secured. The other, in some ways more startling provision, goes beyond most modern constitutions by withdrawing from such amendments four crucial matters: (1) the basic democratic order, (2) the principle of basic rights, (3) the participation of the Laender in legislation, and (4) the federal organization as such. It is clear that these prohibitions (the American Constitution contains only the one about the equal representation of the states in the senate— and that an afterthought) require judicial review for their maintenance. Only if there exists an independent guardian who can stop them will the parliamentary majority (especially a broad consensual one) abstain from disregarding these "fundamental" restrictions as the critics of the Swiss situation have had occasion to point out repeatedly.[28] That the first of these, seemingly a matter of course, should have been included in this list of topics beyond amendment is, of course, due to Hitler's manipulation of the Weimar constitution, and more especially the so-called Enabling Act of March 1933, by which Hitler secured a parliamentary majority for such a basic perversion. On the basis of this act, many German jurists claimed that the Weimar constitution continued to be in force, except for those matters which the Enabling Act had suspended—in point of fact the entire system of responsible parliamentary government which the constitution provided, as well as the entire bill of rights.

These provisions, all traceable to the strong reaction against totalitarian and more especially National Socialist autocracy, provide the setting for the adoption of judicial review in Germany as they did in Italy and Austria. But while this experience was of great weight, it is equally certain that the reason for "the remarkable unanimity" on some sort of judicial review in all three countries (in Austria already practiced since 1920) was that "the exercise of judicial review by the United States Supreme Court has received continued attention in European countries," [29] and indeed that "the impact of Marbury v. Madison was felt in Italy almost a century and a half after the decision." [30] Yet, the argument that this willingness to adopt judicial review was due to American pressure is quite contrary to the facts. The author himself participated in some of the discussions in which actually an unsuccessful effort was made to impress upon Germans the dangers and limitations of judicial review (the Bavarian constitution embodied the earliest of these efforts) related to the notion of "unconstitutional constitutional norms." [31] As a matter of fact, both the Bavarian and the Prussian constitutions of the Weimar period had contained judicial review, and it was therefore clearly an established German inclination to consider judicial review, which in light of 1848 is not surprising. How strong the American impact then had been we have already seen.

But while this impact is striking as far as the general idea of judicial review is concerned, it is largely absent in its implementation. This may be demonstrated by considering two key aspects of the American Supreme Court tradition, one being the method of selecting the judges, and the other the role of the Court in the legal system as a whole. As far as selection of the judges is concerned, the traditional European inclination to leave constitutional interpretation to the legislative bodies, and indeed the presumption in these bodies that they are the ones properly qualified for this task, have led to giving the legislative authorities a major, if not the decisive voice in this selection. In the Federal Republic, all the judges are chosen by the two houses, the Bundestag and the Bundesrat, of which the latter is no true legislative chamber, but an administrative-executive coordinating body (see above, Chapter III). Some of the judges must be career judges, quite a few in fact are law professors (part time), but all of them owe their choice at least in part to party-political considerations. Indeed that trend was so pronounced that at one time each of the two divisions (senates) into which the court was, and is, divided was considered to be dominated by one of the rival parties, and hence were spoken of popularly as the "red" and the "black" senate. In the case of Italy, the partisan perspectives were so strong that it took years even to agree on the method of selecting judges: five being chosen by the judges of the other three highest courts, five by the president, and five by a three-fifths majority of the two houses of parliament sitting together. Endless wranglings over the party positions of various candidates resulted, which were hardly calculated to enhance the legitimacy of the court in the mind of the public. In Austria half of the judges, as well as the presiding judge and his alternate, are appointed by the president of the republic upon being nominated by the government, and the other half are chosen partly by one house, partly by the other.[32] Such choice of the judges by parliamentary bodies is quite at variance with the notion of securing an independent guardian of the constitution and to a considerable extent vitiates the idea of judicial review. The proper procedure under continental European conditions would be a proposal by judicial and university bodies to be acted upon by a relatively neutral representative of the executive establishment, such as the president in each country, if the American precedent of having the chancellor or prime minister propose and the upper house confirm the choice is deemed unworkable, because of the nature of the upper houses in these countries.

But there is another and perhaps even more serious deviation from the American tradition of which the Court's judicial review is a natural expression. It is the unity of the legal order. The Supreme Court has the prime function of insuring that unity. No such function is assigned to the three courts in Germany, Italy, and Austria; several other high courts exist which possess rival jurisdictions. Hence the distinct functional names assigned to these courts entrusted with guarding the constitution: "constitutional court" means that the court is functionally limited to the task of interpreting the constitution. Actually, the very nature of a constitution as the "basic law" of the land tends to invite the assumption of a coordinating and integrating function. But such high courts as the German Supreme Judicial Court, or the Italian Court of Cassation, do not feel bound by the precedents set by the constitutional court as all American courts do, when the Supreme Court has spoken.

This issue was very much discussed in the preparatory convention (preconvention) in 1948 at Herrenchiemsee. A number of key delegates argued in favor of *one* highest court and cited the American experience. The need for unity was repeatedly stressed, and it was pointed out that Germans had neglected the judicial power. It was argued that the third branch needed a distinct and symbolically impressive body to represent it.[33] But this argument was strongly opposed by others. Besides such irrelevant considerations as that a location of several high courts in different cities would link these to the center—an argument which has nonetheless had considerable practical weight— two major positions were taken, namely first that such a single high court would be a mammoth body of 150 to 200 judges, whereas the Supreme Court had only nine old gentlemen, and second that other democratic states, like France and Britain, got along without a single high court. Let us leave aside the second argument as beside the point, since in the name of parliamentary supremacy and legislative "sovereignty" neither country recognizes judicial review. But the first argument is truly amazing in its illogicality. Yet no one argued that the proposal was not to combine all the national courts into one, but that there should be a very small body of last appeal from *all* lower courts. Such a proposition is arguable regardless of whether one accepts case jurisprudence or not; this seems evident enough, but one of the members of the preconvention argued against it on that ground.[34] As a result we must conclude that while the German constitution-makers took over the instrument of judicial review, they did not create the unifying supreme court which is a decisive feature of the American institution.

It is worth noting in this connection that the preconvention sought to reinforce the judicially weakened position of the constitutional court by making the legal effect of its decisions very great; it proposed that decisions of the constitutional court which determine the unconstitutionality of a law possess the force of legislation and must be published in the Law Gazette. In other words, the determination to make the constitution (basic law) be recognized as higher law was very strong, and hence even those opposing a unitary court structure pleaded emphatically for judicial review by a constitutional court.

The same viewpoint became pronounced in France as the debate over the constitution of the Fourth Republic wore on in parliamentary committees that could not reach agreement. In keeping with the postwar disenchantment with the parliaments of the Third and Fourth republics, the French have moved away from strict parliamentarism toward a conception of the constitution as higher law, being shaped by the people rather than the Assembly. Accordingly, the constitutions of 1946 and 1958 have gone considerably further in recognizing an amending power distinct from the ordinary process of making laws. Still the Constitutional Council, which was created in 1958, cannot be considered a constitutional court in the full sense, and it has not exercised any independent judicial review. Unfortunately the secrecy surrounding the preparatory work does not allow us at present to analyze the motivations.[35] It is interesting in this connection to recall that Michel Debré, when presenting the draft constitution to the Conseil d'Etat in 1958, condemned the parliament of the Fourth Republic for its disregard of the constitution "under the pretext of sovereignty, not of the nation (which is right) but of the assemblies (which is fallacious)." He felt that "the creation of the" Constitutional Council "demonstrates the will to subordinate the law, that is the decision of parliament, to the higher rule decreed by the constitution." French politics has however not operated that way, as just observed, and even the propriety of presidential acts of very doubtful constitutionality has not been subjected to judicial scrutiny.[36] The impact of American constitutionalism is illusory here.

The situation is more complex in Italy. We have already pointed out how here too a "politization" of the Constitu-

89

tional Court—already true of the regional Sicilian constitutional court—has occurred and will no doubt continue. Perhaps just for that reason the Italian court has been the most reluctant of the three judicial bodies to get involved in discussions going beyond the strict confines of the constitution. The Italian judges have been most inclined to practice what the Supreme Court has practiced: judicial self-restraint.[37] "Of the three courts, the Italian Court has been the most careful to confine its reasoning narrowly to the provisions of the Constitution and to avoid overt reference to value judgments based on natural law," Professor Taylor Cole has written.[38] The examination of laws and of other measures having the force of law with reference to their compatibility with the Constitution is indeed the acknowledged form of judicial review in the United States. But it leaves room for much argument, and such fighting expressions as "government by judges," "judicial autocracy," and the like have greeted Supreme Court decisions running counter to the decisions of the other two major organs. In the thirties President Roosevelt's program and the majority supporting it were thwarted by a conservative Court "interpreting" or "constructing" the Constitution; in the fifties it was a progressive Court which forced the issue a congressional majority was unwilling to implement, namely the constitutional rights long established for whites, but denied to Negroes.[39] In both situations, the Court rigorously maintained its self-understanding as a careful, rational-legal interpreter.

In Italy, the role of the court as defender of human rights under the constitution is further curtailed by the limitations upon the access of individuals to the court.[40] Thus in dealing with the equality before the law provision, the court argued for wide discretion of the legislature, though it recognized a limit: evident arbitrariness.[41] It is quite clear that judicial review is recognized rather reluctantly in Italy, but that the American example has encouraged the constitution-makers in assigning to courts a definite role in this process. The desire to move in the direction of federalism through the device of regionalism has helped to reinforce this propensity. Such regionalism has been making headway rather slowly, and the Italian Constitutional Court has been much involved in the resulting controversies. To what extent one is here justified in speaking of an American impact is hard to determine. Professor Treves introduces his analysis with the statement cited above about the impact of *Marbury v. Madison*. Yet, as he proceeds to show, the Italian constitution-makers, far from following the American conception of entrusting the judiciary with the task of settling the question of the constitutionality of laws, "out of respect for the supremacy of parliament," created "a special constitutional agency," because "the Constitutional Court does not fit easily into any of the traditional branches of government," and therefore "it would not be proper to place it at the head of the judicial branch." And yet, "the functions of the Court seem to be judicial, or at least prevailingly judicial," since it settles controversies. These controversies are, however, political and therefore "a political qualification is expected from most of the judges, in addition to the technical training." In keeping with this conception of a "constitutional" agency of very particular and limited functions which "require political sensibility," the court is chosen, as we indicated above, from the three different "powers," five each by the executive, the legislative, and the judicial. This agency, the Constitutional Court, "became the guardian of the Constitution." It is held that it does not "impair the function of the judiciary as the guardian of the law." [42]

Another aspect in which the Italians rejected completely

the American conception is in denying individuals the right to plead before the Constitutional Court. Only other courts and public authorities can appeal to it. In such appeals they seek a decision as to whether a legal rule in question is incompatible with a rule of the constitution. An affirmative decision does not "annul" the legal rule, but merely refuses to apply it. Much subtle juristic logic is involved in this and related distinctions which do not interest us here. Suffice it to note that Italian constitution-makers believed they could escape some of the objections to a "government of judges" by these provisions; they also thereby hoped to lighten the load of the court in a country in which the rule of precedent does not apply. It is worth noting for our problem that the American tradition as well as its critics are frequently referred to in these discussions in which Professor Lambert's book is always cited, especially since the great Hauriou adopted the same position, namely that the Supreme Court inhibits social legislation which the majority of the electorate desire.[43] More recent developments hardly justify the view that the Supreme Court prevents social legislation and the implementation of human rights; rather its critics reproach it with unseemly activism and it is indeed true that the Supreme Court has been the pathfinder of progress rather than its inhibitor.[44]

It seems quite evident that while the basic idea of judicial review is of American origin, the particular form it has taken in Italy is much more nearly derived from Austria. Interestingly enough, the Austrians were the first to adopt the idea, after World War I, and it has been maintained there ever since. It was, however, not at all an Austrian idea to consider the court as separate and apart from the judicial system, but rather to treat it as a distinct part of it. In his magistral treatise on Austrian *Staatsrecht*, Professor Adamovich places the Constitutional Court alongside the

Supreme Administrative Court as a body with a highly specialized function, namely that of interpreting the constitution, part of which is the judicial review of acts of the legislative body.[45] Hence as we have seen the Austrian court is chosen half by the executive and half by the legislative branch; in its forty-year history it has rendered valuable service, according to all accounts, in exercising its specialized function. But individuals and private corporate bodies have hardly any standing before it. It functions essentially as an arbiter between various public bodies when they disagree on the meaning of the constitution and as an adviser to the lower courts, when doubts about the constitutionality of legislation arise.[46] This role differs markedly from that of the United States Supreme Court.

We have so far highlighted the issue of judicial review of legislative acts to determine their constitutionality. This issue is, of course, only a small part of the enforcement problem, though highly symptomatic for an advanced stage of the concern with such enforcement. Nevertheless, in the everyday relation of the citizen with his government, the danger that his rights might be infringed arises much more regularly and frequently from the side of the executive than the legislative establishment. And while it is highly desirable, and indeed essential to the functioning of a stable constitutional order, that the legislative body be kept from invading the individual's private sphere without constitutional sanction, it is perhaps even more important that the police and other agencies of the executive be kept within the bounds of law and constitution.

In England, where the constitution is embedded in the general laws, the two tasks become indistinguishable, and only the effective working of the parliamentary system can prevent the parliament, and that means today the governing majority party,[47] from altering those basic rules which in effect are England's constitution. There is no logical reason why it should not be so in other countries. But the probability of their elected representatives exhibiting a comparable self-restraint—and there are in recent years voices of alarm even in England [48]—is by most other people felt to be too small to encourage experimentation along this line, except in traditional Switzerland, which has been discussed above. All courts are, however, called upon to enforce the constitution and in many lands, following the French tradition, administrative courts or councils of state have become the real guardians of the constitutionally guaranteed human rights. This means of course that in terms of concrete effectiveness the Conseil d'Etat is in France today much more important as the constitutional guardian than the Constitutional Council.[49]

After this excursion into the institutional enforcement-machinery problem of human rights, as an area in which the impact of American constitutionalism has become dramatically evident, we want to return briefly to the human rights issues. There can be little question that in all the postwar assemblies particular issues in this field were highlighted by reference to American experience. But the juristic sophistication of those references is not very impressive. In the Herrenchiemsee convention certain articles were cited verbatim, without any reference to the development of the particular article by the Supreme Court. That the original wording was merely the starting point of what became law-in-action in a living constitution was almost totally neglected. Thus the provision against the quartering of troops, which was of course meant to apply to one's own army, was cited and suggested as a way of eliminating the much resented quartering of allied troops in German homes,[50] or the punitive provisions of the Fourteenth Amendment as a basis for a provision dealing with the

Nazis.[51] Altogether the serious tension which exists between granting rights and providing remedies was generally lacking, not only in the German, but also in the Italian, constitutional assembly. As a result, administrative violations of the rights guaranteed in the constitution became so much the order of the day in the fifties that a leading lawyer and scholar could tell the author in an interview that the Italian bill of rights had become "a scrap of paper." [52] It is perhaps worth noting in passing that no organization comparable to the American Civil Liberties Union has made its appearance, in either Italy, Germany, or Austria, not to mention India and the rest, although the American C.L.U. has expended considerable effort through its long-time president, Roger Baldwin, to stimulate interest in such developments.

One idea deserves perhaps a footnote and that is the notion that American troops (and civilians) in peacetime should be guided by the American Constitution and its rights.[53] When first proposed by General Clay, this notion seemed to many of his subordinates very odd. But after a vigorous campaign in which the General took a leading part during the spring and summer of 1948, they gradually fell in line.[54] One important issue in this connection was, of course, the question of whether American personnel should be tried in German courts. In connection with the adoption of the Federal Republic's constitution and its bill of rights in 1949, this issue had to be settled; it was in the final occupation statute, agreed upon among the Allies at Washington in April 1949,[55] for it provided for "respect for the Basic Law" of the emerging new Germany. The position was given final form in the Contractual Agreement of 1952, which was a convention on relations between the three occupying powers and the Federal Republic.[56]

Judicialism, to conclude the foregoing, has been shown

to have had a growing influence, although nowhere has the American system of a Supreme Court which is at the same time a constitutional court and the apex of the judicial system been fully adopted. In view of the functional significance of this institution for American constitutionalism, this fact suggests the limits of the impact of American constitutionalism which were noted also in other fields. Even so, the influence has been considerable, as far as highlighting the crucial importance of effective enforcement procedure for constitutionally guaranteed human rights is concerned. As to these rights themselves, the impact of American ideas is hard to identify because of the extent to which they are part of a common European tradition and constitute part of America's European heritage. Still, in the drive for the adoption of a Universal Declaration of Human Rights the American delegation played a decisive role. The fact that rights are ever more universally recognized even by those who seem least inclined to make them a reality by providing adequate remedies is the distinguishing characteristic of our time. It justifies Americans in the hope that human rights will become more broadly descriptive of the actual behavior of men and governments. The American people themselves have become embroiled in a new revolutionary thrust after the Supreme Court made earnest, in a number of dramatic decisions, of patent implications of the American Constitution and its Bill of Rights. The failure to face these implications over the many generations since the Constitution was adopted surely accounts for the lack of impact of the American Bill of Rights. The Supreme Court's bold insistence that the time has come to make the Constitution and its amendments mean what they say to all Americans may further enhance the impact of the idea of judicialism as an integral part of effective constitutionalism.

NOTES

Chapter I. Reflections on the Influence of American Ideas

1. The general problems of political influence are discussed in Carl J. Friedrich, *Man and His Government* (1963), Ch. 11, but only in terms of personal relations. The influence of ideas is another matter.

2. *Works of John Adams*, Charles Francis Adams, ed. (1851), Vol. V, p. 294. Otto Vossler, in his *Die Amerikanischen Revolutionsideale in ihrem Verhaeltnis zu den europaeischen* (1929), p. 53, cites this passage and comments: "Das zeitgenoessische Urteil der Franzosen ueber die amerikanische Revolution [ist] durch so gut wie gar keine Sachkenntnis getruebt." See also the elaborate documentation of this fact in Bernard Fay, *L'Esprit Révolutionnaire en France et aux Etats Unis à la Fin du XVIIIᵉ Siècle* (1924), p. 102: "Aucune connaissance de première main, aucune documentation sérieuse, beaucoup d'enthousiasme et de la moralité." Fay adds: "Il y'a toute une éclosion de curieux pamphlets mystiques, qui, sous forme de prophétie et en style de l'Apocalypse, président le succès des insurgents, l'élévation de l'Amerique et la déchéance de l'Europe."

3. James Bryce devoted an entire chapter to Tammany Hall (Ch. LXXXVIII in Vol. II of *The American Commonwealth*). See also his chapters on corruption in the big cities, notably LXVII. The most famous muckraker was perhaps Lincoln Steffens whose *The Shame of the Cities* (1904) was a landmark. Less moralizing views, including a functional analysis of corruption, have been set forth more recently. See especially Edward Banfield, *Political Influence* (1961).

4. Sidney and Beatrice Webb, title as cited, pp. 16 ff. and esp. p. 17.

5. Dr. Joseph Priestley, in his fourth letter as published in *Letters to the R.H. Edmund Burke* (1791). He later, after a visit to America, stressed the easiness of change there; see his *Lectures*

on History and General Policy, second ed. (1803), Vol. II, p. 132. These passages are cited by Vossler, p. 58, but to somewhat different purpose.

6. See Fay, *L'Esprit Révolutionnaire,* and Vossler. See also Fay's *Franklin, the Apostle of Modern Times* (1929), esp. Bk. IV.

7. See note 5, above.

8. Tocqueville, *Democracy in America,* Phillips Bradley, ed. (1945), Vol. II, Ch. 21. Melvin Richter has recently given us a very sophisticated analysis of "Tocqueville's Contributions to the Theory of Revolution," in *Nomos,* VIII (1966), 75–121, to which I am much indebted. Louis Hartz, in his well-known *The Liberal Tradition in America* (1955), p. 35, made a rather simplist view the basis of an interpretation which seems radically at variance with the view of the permanent revolution, but is in fact less so than it seems.

9. The theory of the permanent revolution is a complex one. It was made the basis of his interpretation of totalitarianism by Sigmund Neumann, *The Permanent Revolution* (1941); see also my *Man and His Government,* Ch. 35.

10. The problem of systems analysis is coming to be more and more in fashion; for my own view see *ibid.* For an opposed, mechanistic conception cf. David Eastman, *A Systems Analysis of Political Life* (1965).

11. C. J. Friedrich and Robert G. McCloskey, *From the Declaration of Independence to the Constitution—the Roots of American Constitutionalism* (1954), p. VII; the entire introduction provides significant background considerations for the present study.

12. This contrast between a documentary constitution, embodied in one charter, and the British or Israeli kind has been rather misleadingly spoken of as that between a "written" and "unwritten" constitution. Of course, a great part of the British constitution is written. The point is succinctly argued in H. R. G. Greaves, *The British Constitution,* sixth ed. (1958), pp. 15 ff.

13. Greaves, *ibid.,* Introduction.

14. See for a recent authoritative assessment Arthur E. Sutherland, *Constitutionalism in America* (1965).

15. James Kent, *Commentaries on American Law* (1826–1830); Joseph Story, *Commentaries on the Constitution of the United States* (1834).

16. James Bryce's *The American Commonwealth* was first published in 1893; it has gone through many editions, having been completely revised by Lord Bryce in 1910; my references are to the edition of 1924. No more recent work, including even Charles

A. Beard's in many ways remarkable *The Republic* (1943), has been able to achieve comparable stature as a classic.

17. *Constitutional Government and Politics* (1937).

Chapter II. Presidentialism

1. Harold Laski, *The American Presidency* (1940).

2. *The Federalist*, No. 57.

3. Richard E. Neustadt has argued this line in *Presidential Power, the Politics of Leadership* (1960), on the basis of his experience as a participant-observer. A more detached and balanced view is found in Joseph E. Kallenbach, *The American Chief Executive—the Presidency and the Governorship* (1966); this book helpfully brings out the gubernatorial parallels which are so commonly overlooked abroad when the presidency is discussed.

4. See, *e.g.*, George F. Milton's *The Use of the Presidential Power, 1789–1943* (1944).

5. Bryce, Chs. V–VIII. One may note in this connection Harold Laski's critical comments, after duly praising Bryce: "Yet he was also a Gladstonian Liberal, immersed in the special philosophy represented by that experience . . . Bryce accepted the simple faith in liberty of contract . . . He brought with him to America . . . a social philosophy, a way of life, that set the criteria not only of what he was to look for, but also of what he found." Laski, pp. 4–7.

6. See my *Constitutional Government and Democracy* (1950, first ed. 1937), Ch. X. I should like to refer the reader to this book for general background throughout what follows. The particular point here referred to—namely formal recognition of opposition and alternating parties as a form of divided powers—has since been more widely recognized. Note especially the volume recently edited by Robert A. Dahl, *Political Oppositions in Western Democracies* (1965).

7. See my "The New French Constitution in Political and Historical Perspective," *Harvard Law Review*, 72 (March 1959), 801 ff.

8. The problem of totalitarianism is treated extensively in *Totalitarian Dictatorship and Autocracy*, second rev. ed. (1965), esp. Chs. 1 and 2.

9. See the commentary by von Mangoldt (no first name given), *Das Bonner Grundgesetz* (no date given, but published around 1950), pp. 294–295. The deputy Suesterhenn opposed direct election on the basis of experience during 1925–1932. Cf. *Stenographische Berichte*, p. 25; see also pp. 395 ff.

10. *Ibid.*, pp. 397 ff.

11. Kurt Becker, "The Development of Domestic Politics," in *The Politics of Postwar Germany,* Walter Stahl, ed. (1963), pp. 48 ff.

12. Teodosio Marchi, "Il Capo dello Stato," in *Commentario Systematico alla Costituizione Italiana,* Piero Calamandrei and Alessandro Levi, eds. (Firenze, 1950), Vol. II, p. 108.

13. Evarts B. Greene, *The Provincial Governor in the English Colonies of North America* (1898).

14. Max Farrand, *Records of the Federal Convention* (1911 and 1937).

15. *Man and His Government,* Ch. 17.

16. Richard Hiscocks, *The Adenauer Era* (1966).

17. Peter H. Merkl, *Germany: Yesterday and Tomorrow* (1965), p. 249.

18. *The Federalist,* No. 77.

19. Article cited above (n. 7), at pp. 802–803. There is also given a description of the procedure, pp. 806 ff.

20. Clinton Rossiter, *1787—the Grand Convention* (1966), esp. pp. 221–224.

21. Article as cited above (n. 7), at p. 851, n. 25.

22. *Ibid.,* n. 26.

23. Dr. Suesterhenn stated this in the preconvention at Herrenchiemsee, *Sitzungsberichte,* p. 21: "Wir fordern ueber die traditionelle Gewaltenteilung im Sinne Montesquieu's hinaus auch die Gewaltenteilung zwischen Bund und Laendern." See Ch. III, herein, for more detail.

24. Friedrich, *Constitutional Government and Democracy,* Ch. X.

25. Anton Scholl, *Der Einfluss der nordamerikanischen Unionsverfassung auf die Verfassung des Deutschen Reiches vom 28. Maerz 1849* (Borna-Leipzig, 1913), p. 47, citing the deputy, Professor Mittermaier.

26. Veit Valentin, *Geschichte der Deutschen Revolution, 1848–1849,* Vol. II, pp. 572–573.

27. Jose N. Matienzo, *Gobierno Personal y gobierno parlamentario* (La Plata, 1896).

28. Bryce, Vol. I, p. 279.

29. J. N. Matienzo, *Le Gouvernement représentatif fédéral dans la République Argentine* (1912), p. 170. See the entire Ch. IX; he notes that such constitutional fathers as Moreno, Belgrano, and Rivadavia intended to create a parliamentary regime, as practiced in England *and* France; he seems unaware of the radical difference between the two.

30. Justo Arosemena, *Estudios Constitucionales sobre los gobiernos de la América Latina* (1888), Vol. I, p. 380.

31. T. Esquival Obregón, *Influencia de España y los Estados Unidos sobre Mexico* (Madrid, 1918), pp. 41 ff.

32. Bryce, Vol. II, pp. 136 ff. The presidential election then cost a mere 4 million; the latest estimate I have seen was 120 million.

33. T. Varela de Andrade, *América y la revisión constitucional* (Montevideo, 1938).

34. Pedro de Rodrigues Alves, *Genesis da idea republicana no Brasil* (Santiago, 1933).

35. Karl Loewenstein, *Brazil under Vargas* (1945), p. 9. See also more particularly Ruy Barbosa himself, *Comentários à Constituiçao Federal Brasileira* (Sao Paulo, 1932), esp. Vol. III.

36. Herman G. James, *The Constitutional System of Brazil* (1923), esp. Ch. IV.

37. Loewenstein, Ch. II.

38. R. von Mohl, "Recht und Politik der repraesentariven Demokratie," in *Staatsrecht, Voelkerrecht und Politik* (1860), Vol. I, pp. 459 ff.

39. *Ibid.*, p. 465. Mohl there notes the contributions of the Swiss to the general problems, especially Bluntschli, Kaiser, and Cherbulliez.

40. John J. Johnson, ed., *The Role of the Military in Underdeveloped Countries* (1962).

41. Mohl, "Die Weiterentwicklung des demokratischen Prinzips im nordamerikanischen Staatsrecht," *Staatsrecht*, Vol. I, pp. 493–553.

42. *Ibid.*, pp. 500–501.

43. *Ibid.*, pp. 506–509.

44. Henry Steele Commager, in the Introduction to his edition (1946) of Tocqueville.

45. *Ibid.*, pp. 125–143, where the quotes in my text are to be found.

46. Woodrow Wilson, *Congressional Government* (1885), esp. Chs. I and II.

47. See R. Barry Farrell, ed., *Approaches to Comparative and International Politics* (1966); this book includes an article by myself, pp. 97–119, on the subject of the relation of domestic and foreign policy.

48. Friedrich, *Foreign Policy in the Making* (1938).

49. *Democracy in America* (1945 ed.), Vol. I, p. 136.

50. See the historical essay by Philipps Bradley, in his edition of

Tocqueville (1945), Vol. II, pp. 389 ff., where this problem is adumbrated, esp. pp. 403 ff.

51. *Ibid.*, Vol. I, pp. 141–143.

52. Bryce, Chs. V–VIII; in Ch. VIII Bryce attempted a condescending explanation of "why great men are not chosen presidents." It would seem that the American presidency has had a reasonable share of "great men" among its incumbents; it certainly compares satisfactorily with British, French, and German chief executives in this respect. Cf. Bradley, Vol. II, pp. 433 ff.

53. Parlamentarischer Rat, *Verhandlungen des Hauptausschussess*, 32. *Sitzgung* (Jan. 7, 1949), p. 397.

54. Rather misleading is C. Wright Mills, *The Power Elite* (1956), esp. Chs. 8–10. In the mid-1930's, conservatives used to fulminate against the "wonderland of bureaucracy," the "road to serfdom," and similar purple terms.

55. Friedrich, *Constitutional Government and Democracy*, Ch. XIX, and the literature cited there.

56. I am referring to highly regarded political scientists, such as Sir Ivor Jennings and Professor K. C. Wheare; among the states where parliamentary democracy has failed are the Sudan, Pakistan, Nigeria, and Tanzania.

57. *Die Welt* (Nov. 26, 1966).

Chapter III. Federalism

1. Alpheus T. Mason, *Free Government in the Making* (1949); Gottfried Dietze, *The Federalist—a Classic on Federalism and Free Government* (1960).

2. C. J. Friedrich, "Origin and Development of the Concept of Federalism in the United States," in *Jahrbuch des Oeffentlichen Rechts der Gegenwart*, NF, Vol. 9 (1960), pp. 29 ff. See also my more recent report, "Selected Trends and Issues in Contemporary Federal and Regional Relations," in *Status of Puerto Rico* (Government Printing Office, 1966).

3. *E.g.*, see K. C. Wheare, *Federal Government* (1946). The English term "federal government" is on the Continent usually rendered as *état fédéral, Bundesstaat*, etc.

4. Besides the report cited in note 2 above, see "New Tendencies in Federal Theory and Practice," in *Jahrbuch des Oeffentlichen Rechts der Gegenwart*, Vol. 14 (1965), pp. 1–14.

5. Otto von Gierke, *The Development of Political Theory*, tr. Bernard Freyd (1939), Ch. V, pp. 257 ff.

6. C. J. Hughes, *Confederacies* (Leicester University Press, 1963); E. C. Burnett, *The Continental Congress* (1941).

7. Rossiter, *1787—the Grand Convention*; he includes a good bibliography.

8. Friedrich, *Constitutional Government and Democracy*, Ch. VIII.

9. For the communitarian analysis see the two papers cited above, note 4.

10. See, *e.g.*, *Le Fédéralisme* (1956), esp. contributions by Georges Vedel and Andre Mathiot, pp. 31 ff. and 241 ff. (This valuable book, published for the Centre des Sciences Politiques de Nice of the Université d'Aix-Marseille, gives no editor; it is the work of many authors.)

11. Arthur E. Sutherland, *Constitutionalism in America* (1965), p. 384.

12. David B. Truman, "Federalism and the Party System," in Arthur W. MacMahon, *Federalism—Mature and Emergent* (1955), pp. 115–136.

13. As quoted in William E. Rappard, *La Constitution de la Confédération Suisse, 1848–1948* (1948), p. 134.

14. *Ibid.*, p. 133.

15. *Ibid.*, p. 138.

16. On the importance of this see Robert R. Bowie's study "The Federal Legislature," in *Studies in Federalism*, Bowie and Friedrich, eds. (1954), pp. 3–28, esp. pp. 8 ff.

17. Rappard, pp. 143–144.

18. *Ibid.*, pp. 268–269.

19. *Stenographische Berichte ueber die Verhandlungen der deutschen constitutierenden Nationalversammlung zu Frankfurt am Main*, Franz Wigard, ed. (Leipzig, 1848), cited hereafter as *Verhandlungen, Frankfurt,* followed by volume and page.

20. *Ibid.*, IV, 2,743.

21. *Ibid.*, 2,724.

22. *Ibid.*, 2,726.

23. *Ibid.*, 2,728, 2,736, 2,740.

24. *Ibid.*, 2,727.

25. See esp. Mohl, as cited above, note 38, Ch. II.

26. Matienzo, *Le Gouvernement . . . Argentine*, p. 69: "Avec ces differences de forme et de temps c'est le même procès sus d'organisation qu'ont suivi les Etats-Unis, la Suisse et l'Allemagne . . . et qui finira par donner un gouvernement fédéral à toutes les nations civilisées."

27. *Ibid.*, Ch. IV. See also Louis V. Varela, *Historia Constitucional de la República Argentina* (1910), Vol. III, Chs. 5–

28. See, *e.g.*, the very influential book by J. B. Alberdi, *Las Bases y puntos de partida para la organización política de la Repúb-*

lica Argentina (1852); in this work the factors making for unity and those making for diversity are soberly juxtaposed, and the conclusion is drawn (see esp. Ch. XV), culminating in the demand for a conciliation of "las libertades de cada provincia y las prerogativas de toda la nación," which Alberdi calls an "inevitable solution." Cf. Arosemena, *Estudios Constitucionales* . . . , Vol. I, pp. 189 ff.

29. Obregón, *Influencia de España*.

30. Arosemena, *Estudios Constitucionales*, Vol. II, pp. 504 ff., esp. p. 507.

31. Obregón, p. 999.

32. Herman G. James, *The Constitutional System of Brazil* (1923), p. 12.

33. Barbosa, *Comentários* . . . , Vol. I, p. v. For examples see Vol. I, pp. 40, 45, 52, and more esp. p. 57: "o congresso liberal . . . adopton o regimen federativo, copiando o sen programma da constitução americana." Similar references are found throughout the work.

34. Loewenstein, p. 15.

35. Luis Sanchez Agesta, *Curso de Derecho Constitucional Comparado* (1963), pp. 235 ff. and literature cited on p. 239.

36. The relevant constitutional provisions are in Argentina's constitution of 1853, Arts. 67 and 104; in Mexico's of 1857, Arts. 72, 75, and 117; in Brazil's of 1891, Art 18.

37. S. V. Linares Quintana, *Teoria y práctica del Estado federal* (1942); *Tratado de la Ciencia de Derecho Constitucional Argentino y comparado* (1963), Vol. IX; Zorraquin Becú, *El federalismo argentino* (1939); M. Cavalcanti de Carvalho, *Las Constituciones de los Estados Unidos del Brasil* (1958); R. Gallardo, *Las Constituciones de la República federal de Centro-américa* (Madrid, 1958).

38. Admittedly, around this issue a vast and complicated historical controversy has raged. Professor Robert C. Binkley has summed it up well in his *Realism and Nationalism—1852–1871* (1935), p. 294: "whether it was brought on by the French or by the Prussians, certainly it is evident that in both countries ministers who enjoyed the confidence of popularly elected parliaments welcomed the appeal to arms."

39. Rupert Emerson, *State and Sovereignty in Modern Germany* (1928), Ch. III.

40. *Lord Durham's Report on the Affairs of British North America,* ed. with introd. by Sir C. P. Lucas, 3 vols. (1912).

41. Edward A. Freeman, *A History of Federal Government in Greece and Italy* (1863), did not really deal with the modern concept at all. He disguised his failure to comprehend the issue behind

the remark that "the exact definition, both of a federation in general and the particular forms of federation, has often taxed the ingenuity of both political philosophers and international lawyers."

42. Alexander Brady, *Democracy in the Dominions* (1948), p. 39.

43. J. A. Corry and Henry J. Abraham, *Elements of Democratic Government* fourth ed. (1964), pp. 163 ff.

44. See my report, cited in n. 2, section IX, C.; also, for greater detail, the very impressive official *Preliminary Report of the Royal Commission on Bilingualism and Biculturalism* (Ottawa, 1965).

45. Alfred Deakin, as quoted by Brady, p. 142, n. 3.

46. E. M. Hunt, *American Precedents in Australian Federation* (1930), p. 163.

47. C. J. Friedrich and Robert H. Guttman, "The Federal Executive," in *Studies in Federalism*, Bowie and Friedrich, eds., pp. 63–93. See also my report cited in *ibid.*, n. 2, Section V.

48. Karl Heinz Neunreither, *Der Bundesrat zwischen Politik und Verwaltung* (1959); and his English summary in "Politics and Bureaucracy in the West German *Bundesrat*," *The American Political Science Review*, LIII (1959), 713–731.

49. Hugo Preuss, *Staat, Recht und Freiheit* (1926), pp. 368 ff.

50. For this argument and its complexities, *Constitutional Government and Democracy*, Ch. XI.

51. For a participant-observer's assessment, see Arnold Brecht, *Aus Naechster Naehe, Lebenserinnerungen eines Beteiligten Beobachters 1884–1927* (1966), Ch. 48, and his general analysis in *Federalism and Regionalism in Germany* (1945).

52. Clarence Streit, *Union Now* (1938); E. H. Carr, *Twenty Years Crisis* (1939); and my own *Foreign Policy in the Making*.

53. Gerard J. Mangone, *The Idea and Practice of World Government* (1951); the very extensive literature is to some considerable extent cited here. For an interesting recent study, sophisticated and constitutionalist, Grenville Clark and Louis P. Sohn, *World Order through World Law* (1958).

54. Klaus von Beyme, "Federal Theory and Party Reality in the Soviet Union," *Public Policy*, Montgomery and Smithies, eds., XIII (1964), 395–412.

55. Franz Neumann, "Federalism and Freedom: A Critique," in MacMahon, pp. 44–57; Laski, in *The American Presidency*, is similarly inclined. See also the statements by Lenin as cited in Julian Towster, *Political Power in the U.S.S.R.—1917–1948* (1948), p. 62: "We are against federation on principle, it weakens the economic ties."

56. Towster, *ibid.*, p. 63, n. 41.

57. Von Beyme, "Federal Theory," and Friedrich, *Totalitarian Dictatorship*.

58. Edward H. Litchfield, ed., *Governing Postwar Germany* (1953), esp. Chs. 1, 4, and 5. See also Peter H. Merkl, *The Origin of the West German Republic* (1962), esp. pp. 28 ff., and the official document, Office of Military Government, U.S. Civil Administration Division, *Documents on the Creation of the German Federal Constitution* (Berlin, 1949), *passim*. I believe Merkl is right in saying that "a glance at the literature of the period reveals that the striking consensus for a German return to federalism antedates 1945."

59. Merkl, p. 28.

60. The phrase "reasonably equal" ought not to be interpreted, as it so often is, in terms of the largest and the smallest unit but in terms of the series. It is the difference between each successive unit that matters. For this point, *Constitutional Government and Democracy*, Ch. XI.

61. The *Protokolle* contain only ten explicit references to the U.S. Constitution, and most of these concern special technical points, such as the provisions for forming new states, the staffing of senatorial offices, their inadequate pay, and so forth. One fundamental point is made, namely that in the U.S., Brazil, and Mexico the states are thought of as pre-existing, antecedent to the federal union, whereas in Germany they acted merely as trustees for the nation—a strange position to take in view of the long history of many of the German states; *e.g.*, there was a Bavaria before the discovery of America. Altogether, this issue and that of the senate are the primary concerns, as far as American federalism is concerned. The references are as follows: *Protokolle des Unterausschusses*, I and II, pp. 98 and 205; *ibid.*, II, pp. 20, 22, 29, 31; *Vollsitzungen*, A, pp. 14, 19, 88; B, pp. 5 and 12.

62. U.S. Department of State, *Germany, 1947–1949, the Story in Documents*, pp. 75 ff., gives the texts of these proposals which had been worked out in a conference during May 1948. See also Litchfield.

63. See for this Parlamentarischer Rat, 2. Sitzung, 8. IX (1948), *Berichte*, p. 18. Dr. Suesterhenn is referring to an informal statement made by the author, who was the only Allied official consulted during the Herrenchiemsee convention, which was held in strictest seclusion from all Allied interference on an island in a Bavarian lake, the Chiemsee, east of Munich.

64. Professor K. V. Rao, in his *Parliamentary Democracy in India* (1961), p. 270, reports Dr. Ambedkar as comparing the Indian

constitution with the U.S. one, but commenting that "the differences that distinguish them are more fundamental and glaring than the similarities between the two." Indian federalism, Rao added, is a combination of all the factors that make for federalism. See his entire Ch. IX. A similar analysis is offered by Professor N. Srinivasan, *Democratic Government in India* (1954), pp. 145 ff., who even at that early date insisted that "the federal character of the Constitution is indisputable." It has of course become more patent every year.

65. See, for this aspect of the matter, the three reports of the Hague conferences, as well as the flood of publications of the various organizations federated in the "European Movement." For an appraisal, see, *e.g.*, the several articles in C. Grove Haines, ed., *European Integration* (1957).

66. Bowie and Friedrich, *Studies in Federalism* was first prepared at the request of Paul-Henri Spaak and the preparatory commission for the Assemblée Ad Hoc, called upon to develop a draft for a constitution of a European Political Community; it was submitted by Spaak to the Council of Ministers of the Council of Europe in 1953. See for this the introduction to the above volume which also contains the draft. It is the most explicit document showing the impact of American constitutionalism upon the unification plans. But this impact is already apparent in the first Hague Conference, May 1948, and continues to manifest itself in the vast literature on the subject of European unification.

67. Ernst B. Haas, *The Uniting of Europe, Political, Social, and Economic Forces, 1950–1957* (1958).

68. George Liska, *Europe Ascendant—the International Politics of Unification* (1964).

69. Altiero Spinelli, *Manifesto dei Federalisti Europei* (1957); the same, *Rapporto sull'Europa* (1965), esp. Ch. 6; Alexandre Marc, *L'Europe dans le Monde* (1965), esp. pp. 202 ff.

Chapter IV. The Judicial Power and Human Rights

1. On the evolution of human rights in general see my *Transcendant Justice—the Religious Dimension of Constitutionalism* (1964), Ch. V: "Rights, Liberties, Freedoms—the Humanist Core of Constitutionalism." On the background, see also Friedrich and McCloskey, *From the Declaration*. Interesting special aspects are treated in Benjamin F. Wright, *Consensus and Continuity—1776–1787* (1958), pp. 51 ff., and David Fellman, *Religion in American Public Law* (1965), esp. pp. 9 ff.

2. Zechariah Chafee, Jr., in *Three Human Rights in the Constitu-*

tion (1956), discussed three rights found in the original document, prior to amendment, namely freedom of debate in Congress, the prohibition of bills of attainder, and the freedom of movement. On the contract clause Benjamin F. Wright, *The Contract Clause* (1938).

3. Out of the vast literature one might mention as a broad survey Robert E. Cushman, *Civil Liberties in the United States* (1956). See also in the European (French) perspective *Chrestomathie des Droits de l'Homme,* a special issue of *Politique—Revue Internationale des Doctrines et des Institutions* (1960), edited by M. Prelot and B. Mirkine-Guetzevich.

4. Georg Jellinek, *Die Erklaerung der Menschen—und Buergerrechte* (1895), fourth ed. (1927), Ch. III; English ed. by Max Farrand (1901). Jellinek cites in his notes a number of further works, among which I would want to mention G. L. Scherger, *The Evolution of Modern Liberty* (1904), esp. pp. 210 ff.; Klövekorn, *Entstehung der Erklaerung der Menschen—und Buergerrechte* (1911); and W. Rees, *Erklaerung der Menschen—und Buergerrechte* (1912). The criticism by Emil Boutmy, "La Déclaration des droits de l'homme et du citoyen et M. Jellinek," in *Etudes Politiques* (1907), pp. 119 ff., has not been accepted by authoritative French scholarship, which has followed A. Aulard, *Histoire politique de la Révolution française* (1901), pp. 19 ff. See for a masterly recent discussion of the general issue R. R. Palmer, *The Age of the Democratic Revolution* (1959), Vol. I, Ch. IX. For the French translation of American state constitutions see *Recueil des lois constitutives des colonies anglaises . . .* (1778) (Switzerland). Palmer, in Appendix IV, *The Age,* offers a comparison, article by article, of the Virginia and French declarations.

5. *Mémoires du General Lafayette* (1837), Vol. II, p. 46.

6. Farrand, *Records of the Federal Convention,* Vol. II, p. 588; see also the brief comment in Rossiter, pp. 226–227.

7. *Ibid.,* pp. 302–305.

8. On the background documentation see Oscar and Mary Handlin, *The Popular Sources of Political Authority—Documents of the Massachusetts Convention, 1780* (1966).

9. Brady, pp. 58 ff., 161 ff.; E. M. Hunt, pp. 212–221.

10. See Friedrich, *Constitutional Government and Democracy,* pp. 161 ff.

11. See Paolo Barile, "La Revisione della Costituzione," in Calamandrei and Levi, Vol. II, pp. 465–496.

12. A. de Tocqueville, Vol. I, pp. 269 ff. On Mill, see "Liberty," *Nomos,* IV (1962), esp. Chs. 5–10.

13. It has been argued that these were not truly "rights." The

argument cogently stresses their difference from the older individual rights, but fails to bring forward convincing reasons for not considering such propositions as the "right to work" rights. For the argument, see Maurice Cranston, *What Are Human Rights?* (1962). Georges Burdeau, in his *Traité de Science Politique* (1953), Vol. V, pp. 556 ff., takes the same position. Positively, the fact that these rights" are contained in numerous bills of rights, both parochial and universal, suggests that there must be a rightlike aspect to these newer claims of equality. See my article cited in note 1, above.

14. Agesta, *Curso de Derecho Constitucional Comparado*, pp. 207 ff., speaks of "el regimen juridico de la libertad" in discussing the judicial power.

15. *The Federalist*, No. 78.

16. See Sutherland; Robert M. McCloskey, *The American Supreme Court* (1960); Edward S. Corwin, *John Marshall and the Constitution* (1921); Robert H. Jackson, *The Struggle for Judicial Supremacy* (1941); for a comparative overview, Edward McWhinney, *Judicial Review in the English-Speaking World*, second rev. ed. (1960).

17. For a recent philosophical restatement of this position, see L. A. Hart, *The Concept of Law* (1961); for an earlier assessment, Sir C. K. Allen, *Law in the Making*, sixth rev. ed. (1958).

18. Léon Duguit, *Droit Constitutionel* (1927), Vol. I; Fritz Fleiner, *Schweizerisches Bundesstaatsrecht* (1932), pp. 442 ff.; Fleiner, *Schweizerische und Deutsche Staatsauffassung* (1929), pp. 16 f.

19. Donald G. Morgan, *Congress and the Constitution* (1966).

20. *Verhandlungen, Frankfurt*, Vol. VIII, p. 5,690.

21. Robert von Mohl, *Das Bundesstaatsrecht der Vereinigten Staaten von Nord-amerika* (sic) (1824). Judicial review is discussed on pp. 298–299. In his memoirs Mohl rather deprecates this, his early and very influential work, as rather *"duerftig"* (inadequate) compared with Tocqueville, Kent, and others, his main objection being that it was done from books only.

22. Duguit, Vol. V, p. 3,651.

23. *Ibid.*, pp. 3,614–3,615.

24. See my "The Issue of Judicial Review in Germany," *Political Science Quarterly*, XLIII (1928), 188 ff. For further background, see Gottfried Dietze, "America and Europe—Decline and Emergence of Judicial Review," *Virginia Law Review*, 44 (1958), 1,233 ff.

25. Santos P. Amadeo, *Argentine Constitutional Law—the Judi-*

cial Function in the Maintenance of the Federal System and the Preservation of Individual Rights (1943), p. viii. This work builds a solid argument, supported by many cases.

26. Ibid., p. 163.

27. Ibid., p. 216; the next two quotes on p. 217.

28. Both Fleiner and Rappard.

29. Taylor Cole, "Three Constitutional Courts: A Comparison," The American Political Science Review, LIII (1959), 963 ff., at p. 967; see also the same author's "The West German Federal Constitutional Court: An Evaluation after Six Years," The Journal of Politics, 20 (1958), 278 ff.

30. Giuseppino Treves, "Judicial Review of Legislation in Italy," Journal of Public Law, 7 (1958), 345 ff., at p. 345. However, in the digest of the preparatory discussions, La Costituzione della Repubblica Italiana, Falzone, Palermo and Cosentino, eds. (n.d.), pp. 240 ff., no such "impact" is to be observed; only one reference, and that negative, is reported there, p. 240 (Nitti).

31. See for this perplexing issue Gottfried Dietze, "Unconstitutional Constitutional Norms? Constitutional Development in Postwar Germany," Virginia Law Review, 42 (1956), 1 ff.

32. See Ludwig Adamovich, Grundriss des Österreichischen Staatsrechts (1947), 220 ff. See also the commentary by Cole, "Three Constitutional Courts."

33. Protokolle des Unterausschusses, III, pp. 63 ff. and 151 ff. The Deputies Küster, Zürcher, and Carl Schmid argued the case.

34. The gifted Dr. Brill (Hesse) in the third plenary session, Protokolle, pp. 11–13.

35. See my article "The New French Constitution in Political and Historical Perspective," Harvard Law Review, 72 (1959), 801 ff.

36. Roy C. Macridis and Bernard E. Brown, The de Gaulle Republic (1960); for the Fourth Republic, Georges Burdeau, Manuel de Droit Public (1948); Maurice Duverger, Manuel de Droit Constitutionel, fifth ed. (1948).

37. Edward McWhinney, Constitutionalism in Germany and the Federal Constitutional Court (1962), pp. 31 ff., has dealt with this complex matter.

38. Cole, "Three Constitutional Courts," p. 974.

39. It is revealing to find that Mohl, the influential commentator on the American Constitution (see above, note 21), writing in 1824 divided the discussion of human rights under the American Constitution into three headings: rights for whites, rights for freed blacks, and rights of slaves.

40. See Treves, "Judicial Review of Legislation in Italy." Most books on contemporary Italy discuss this problem; *e.g.*, Dante Germino and Stefano Passigli, *The Government and Politics of Contemporary Italy* (to be published in 1968).

41. Treves, pp. 345 ff. See also the discussions in *Atti della Commissione per la Costituzione,* Vol. I, pp. 243–248. In this connection, the study by Salvatore Catinella, *La Corte Suprema federale nel sistema costituzionale degli Stati Uniti d'America* (1954), pp. 89–130, is worth comparing; it proves an awareness of the differences on the part of the Italians; cf. also Paolo Barile, *Corso di Diritto Costituzionale* (1962), pp. 123 ff. and 167 ff.

42. Treves, p. 346.

43. Michele Petrucci, "La Corte Costituzionale," in Calamandrei and Levi, Vol. I, pp. 436 ff. The author acknowledges the influence which the American system has exercised.

44. Dietze, "America and Europe," pp. 1,268 ff., takes the view that the Supreme Court has abdicated and hopes that European courts will not follow the American example, but that rather "it may cross again the Atlantic."

45. Adamovich, pp. 293–316.

46. See Cole "Three Constitutional Courts," and Dietze, "America and Europe."

47. See, *inter alia*, Greaves, Ch. 1; it is symptomatic that an able analysis of party politics in Britain, Samuel H. Beer, *British Politics in the Collectivist Age* (1965), should not find it necessary to deal with the issue, except marginally, *e.g.*, when discussing the Tory view, etc.

48. For an extreme example see the distinguished jurist G. W. Keeton, *The Passing of Parliament* (1952).

49. The Conseil d'Etat publishes, since 1947, annual *Etudes et Documents,* which are rich in detailed documentation; see, *e.g.*, 1961, pp. 11 ff. and 53 ff. The same volume contains also, as do all of them, a part (II) devoted to reports of the several sections of the Conseil d'Etat; finally, on p. 251 there is a report on a special meeting held at Heidelberg on constitutional courts. See for commentary on the work of the Conseil, Georges Langrod, *Some Current Problems of Administration in France Today* (San Juan, 1961), Ch. III.

50. *Protokolle des Unterausschusses,* I, p. 129.

51. *Ibid.,* p. 164; see also for other illustrations, p. 137, and *ibid.,* II, p. 10.

52. Considering the Italian jurists cited above, such as Barile, this statement was undoubtedly somewhat extreme.

53. House Report 1845, 80th Congress, May 1, 1948, entitled *Final Report on Foreign Aid* (Herter Committee Report), pp. 113 ff., esp. at 136 ff.

54. Lucius D. Clay, *Decision in Germany* (1950), pp. 412 ff.

55. Litchfield, *Governing Postwar Germany*, esp. pp. 44 ff.

56. Merkl, *The Origin of the West German Republic*, pp. 172 ff.